Contents

Part Three · Assessment

Part Four · Documents

Maps

Introduction to the Series

The seminar method of teaching is being used increasingly in VI forms and at universities. It is a way of learning in smaller groups through discussion, designed both to get away from and to supplement the basic lecture techniques. To be successful, the members of a seminar must be informed, or else—in the unkind phrase of a cynic, it can be a 'pooling of ignorance'. The chapter in the textbook of English or European history by its nature cannot provide material in this depth, but at the same time the full academic work may be too long and perhaps too advanced for students at this level.

For this reason we have invited practising teachers in universities, schools and colleges of further education to contribute short studies on specialised aspects of British and European history with these special needs and pupils of this age in mind. For this series the authors have been asked to provide, in addition to their basic analysis, a full selection of documentary material of all kinds and an up-to-date and comprehensive bibliography. Both these sections are referred to in the text, but it is hoped that they will prove to be valuable teaching and learning aids in themselves.

Note on the System of References:

A bold number in round brackets (**5**) in the text refers the reader to the corresponding entry in the Bibliography section at the end of the book.

A bold number in square brackets, preceded by 'doc.' [**docs 6, 8**] refers the reader to the corresponding items in the section of Documents, which follows the main text.

PATRICK RICHARDSON
General Editor

Preface

I am grateful to P. Clark who has very kindly allowed me to use material from his thesis on Kentish Urban Society relating to Maidstone and Canterbury and to D. Palliser who has made available material from his thesis on Tudor York; to J. F. Pound who provided me with information on the Southertons of Norwich, and to Cambridge University Press who previously published the map showing *Wyatt's Rebellion* in 'Two Tudor Conspiracies' by D. M. Loades.

I am much indebted to a number of friends, who have read sections of the book in typescript and made useful comments and suggestions: P. Clark, M. J. Kitch, R. I. Moore, D. Palliser, C. S. R. Russell, E. F. Russell and N. R. N. Tyacke. I would particularly like to thank P. B. Richardson for his interest and assistance throughout the writing of this book.

I would also like to thank my pupils at King's College School, Wimbledon for the stimulus they have provided in discussions of Tudor Rebellions. They have been tolerant of my preoccupation with the subject. P. R. Engeham and F. A. K. Yasamee have read a number of chapters and made suggestions. M. T. Meteyard planned the maps of the Pilgrimage of Grace 1536 and the Northern Rebellion 1569. C. D. Barnett drew the map of the Western Rebellion 1549. M. T. Meteyard's criticism of an early draft of Chapter 8, The Northern Rebellion 1569, and his subsequent research on the rebellion, caused me to modify considerably my interpretation of its causes. The final form of this chapter owes much to his own research.

My greatest debt is to my wife for her patient help and encouragement.

Note to Second Edition

I have taken the opportunity provided by a new impression to make some additions to the bibliography and a few corrections. Much important work on the Pilgrimage of Grace has appeared since this book was written and I have revised my account of it in a few places in the light of the research that has been published. Mr M. E. James and Dr R. B. Smith, in complementary studies of the Lincolnshire rising and the rising in the West Riding, have brought together an impressive amount of circumstantial evidence to support the view that the Pilgrimage was a movement mobilised and led by nobility, gentry and clergy rather than a spontaneous rising by the commons. Our understanding of what happened has taken a leap forward as a result of these two attempts to look behind the version of events given by the men who had rebelled. Dr Smith has stressed the ambiguous behaviour of Lord Darcy, the Nevills, the Percies and Archbishop Lee and has convincingly related the geography of the revolt to the pattern of territorial lordship in the north. Mr James has emphasised how dependent the Lincolnshire movement was on a 'powerful clerical initiative' in the first place and on gentry leadership thereafter. Other studies support the same picture. Dr Bowker has devoted a paper to examining the crucial role of the clergy in Lincolnshire. Dr Haigh has discussed the close liaison between the monks and the commons in Lancashire. The wider question of the motives of the rebels has meanwhile remained a matter of debate. In general surveys Professor Dickens on the one hand has argued that the Pilgrimage should be seen as a predominantly secular movement, while Dr Davies on the other has claimed that 'religious factors were an essential feature of the Pilgrimage'. His discussion of the role of religion in causing the rebellion, giving it cohesion and legitimating resistance to the King seems to me to be important. In the same context Dr Haigh's conclusion that 'in Lancashire the rebels were more concerned with religious than economic issues' and Dr Bowker's stress on religion should be noted.

Finally on the Pilgrimage, Dr Bush has questioned the interpretation which has normally been given to the relationships between the Henrician Government, the Duke of Norfolk and northern gentry in the period of its aftermath, in the light of a reconsideration of the Tudor approach to the whole problem of the defence of the northern border.

Two other substantial new works deal with Tudor rebellions. Professor Jordan has provided narratives and some analysis of the two major rebellions of 1549 in his study of Edward VI. He has taken a rather more severe view than I did, perhaps too severe a view, of Lord Russell's conduct of the campaign against the western rebels. Professor MacCaffrey has devoted a chapter to the northern rebellion of 1569 in his book on the early years of the Elizabethan regime.

SHEFFIELD

ANTHONY FLETCHER

July 1972

Part One

BACKGROUND

1 The Tudor Theory of Obligation

Tudor governments, lacking military forces with which to maintain order and obedience, needed a generally accepted theory of obligation. Their need for such a theory was increased by the changes of the 1530s and the dangers attending on them. The Henrician government knew of the events at Munster and were aware of the social and political implications of Anabaptism. The break from Rome brought an immediate suggestion from Chapuys, the Imperial Ambassador, optimistic about the chances of civil war in the country, to his master: 'It can hardly displease you to make an enterprise against this kingdom.' In 1538 Cardinal Pole tried to arrange a crusade of Christian princes against Henry VIII. All those, whether Erasmians or Lutherans, who wanted reform of the Church at that time rested their hopes in the King as Supreme Head.

For all these reasons Thomas Cromwell saw the necessity of organising and directing a group of publicists to elaborate on the theory of non-resistance expressed by William Tyndale in his *Obedience of a Christian Man* (**2, 48, 90**). He maintained close control of the printing presses, thus almost entirely suppressing counter-propaganda and in 1538 the import of English books printed abroad was banned. The arguments deployed by the Henrician publicists, men like Richard Morrison, Thomas Starkey and Robert Barnes, were taken up by those who replied to the rebels of 1549: Sir John Cheke, Thomas Cranmer and Nicholas Udall [**docs 10, 14**]. The pamphlets and ballads of Elizabeth's reign continued to echo the same themes (**20**). An account of the Tudor theory of obligation based on these writers will show how they reflected and emphasised the main elements of the Tudor world picture.

A recent analysis of the arguments for religious unity in England in the period 1530–1650 has shown that all moral sense and political obligation was believed to depend in the last resort on religion, by which 'the whole of society was thought to be sanctioned' (**73**).

Religion was the prime cohesive force of Tudor society [**doc. 19**].
As Richard Hooker said:

> Men fearing God are thereby a great deal more effectively than by
> politic laws restrained from doing evil; inasmuch as those laws
> have no further power than over our outward actions only,
> whereas unto men's inward cogitations, unto the privy interests
> and motions of their hearts, religion serveth for a bridle.

The Royal Supremacy implied the identification of church and state.
The purpose of the doctrine of the Godly Prince, elaborated by
Tudor writers, was to assert, in Richard Taverner's words, that
kings 'represent unto us the person even of God himself'.

The theory of obligation employed most frequently was that of
Romans 13: 'The powers that be are ordained of God.' Thus Sir
John Cheke in the *Hurt of Sedition* was able to denounce the rebels
of 1549 as sinning first against God, second against the King. The
doctrine was one of non-resistance rather than obedience because
it was usually qualified by a paraphrase of Peter's statement in
Acts 5:29 that 'We ought to obey God rather than men'. Robert
Barnes maintained that powers must be suffered 'always provided
that they repugn not against the Gospel nor destroy our faith'. But
little emphasis was put on this qualification. It was much more common to stress, as Latimer did in one of his sermons, that it might be
the will of God that a sinful man should suffer under tyrants.

> If the king should require of thee an unjust request, yet art thou
> bound to pay it and not to resist and rebel . . . the king indeed is
> in peril of his soul for asking of an unjust request; and God will in
> His due time reckon with him for it: but thou must not take upon
> thee to judge him. . . . And know this, that whensoever there is
> any unjust exaction laid upon thee it is a plague and punishment
> for thy sin.

But the powers that be were not just political. Every man, whether
apprentice, journeyman or tenant, and every woman and child
was expected to obey their immediate superior. 'The rule of
obedience', said Archbishop Whitgift, 'that is betwixt the magistrate
and the subject holdeth betwixt the husband and the wife, the
father and his child, the master and the servant.' It is this idea which
connects the theory of obligation, based on *Romans*, with the doctrine
of the Great Chain of Being, the most persuasive foundation for a

theory of non-resistance available to the Tudor writer. The idea of the Great Chain of Being has seldom been better expressed than by the fifteenth-century jurist Sir John Fortescue:

> God created as many different kinds of things as he did creatures, so that there is no creature which does not differ in some respect superior or inferior to all the rest. So that from the highest angel down to the lowest of his kind there is absolutely not found an angel that has not a superior and inferior; nor from man down to the meanest worm is there any creature which is not in some respect superior to one creature and inferior to another. So that there is nothing which the bond of order does not embrace.

That the Great Chain of Being existed was a commonplace assumption of those who lived in Tudor England. The metaphor 'served to express the unimaginable plentitude of God's creation, its unfaltering order and its ultimate unity' (42). This was a society that in its outlook on the world and the cosmos remained impeccably traditional. The principle of degree dominated men's imaginations. Order among men corresponded to the order of the cosmos. Shakespeare assumed the interconnections of 'the heavens themselves, the planets and this centre'; in each he saw hierarchy and place.

> How could communities,
> Degrees in schools and brotherhoods in cities,
> Peaceful commerce from dividable shores,
> The primogeniture and due of birth,
> Prerogative of age, crowns, sceptres, laurels,
> But by degree stand in authentic place?

asked Ulysses in his great speech on degree in *Troilus and Cressida*.

The Great Chain of Being meant interdependence as well as authority; all authorities in it held their power for the good of their inferiors and subject to their superiors. As William Gouge said:

> They that are superiors to some are inferiors to others . . . The master that hath servants under him, may be under the authority of a magistrate. Yea, God hath so disposed every one's several place, as there is not any one, but in some respect is under another, and all under the king. The king himself is under God.

This was why, as Protector Somerset explained to the western rebels, there must be a difference between 'the harte and wordes of a king enoincted that ruleth by counsell and kepeth his Realme in defence and quyetnes' and the 'blinde guides of Sedicon and uprore'. The ideal was one of harmony and cooperation: 'We are all members of one body; and we know we have need one of another. The Lord cannot want the help of the toe, though the least and lowest member', wrote Edwin Sandys. The image of the commonwealth as a human body was a favourite one with Tudor publicists (**82,** p. 295). Morrison used it to show the absurdity of rebellion and explained that it was for the welfare of society as a whole that while some must rule others must work: 'These must not go, arme in arme, but the one before, the other behynde' [**doc. 10**]. Here as so often in Tudor political writing Morrison was paraphrasing and expanding on a biblical passage, in this case *1 Corinthians* 12:12.

Rebellion upset both the social and the political order. 'God hath made the pore, and hath made them to be poore', wrote Cheke, 'that he myght shew his might, and set them aloft when he listeth, for such cause as to hym seemeth and plucke downe the riche, to hys state of povertie to shew his power.' 'Where there is any lack of order', said Sir Thomas Elyot, 'needs must be perpetual conflict.' The Great Chain theory was strongly reflected in the *Homily of Obedience*, issued and ordered to be read in churches in 1547: 'Where there is no right order there reigneth all abuse, carnal liberty, enormity, sin and babylonical confusion' (**14,** p. 15).

It can be seen that rebellion offended the deepest assumptions of the age; at its crudest and most exaggerated government propaganda appealed to the dread of anarchy with which men were obsessed. The *Homily of Obedience* described the 'mischief and utter destruction' that would ensue without kings and magistrates: 'No man shall sleep in his house or bed unkilled.' Nicholas Udall pointed out to the western rebels in 1549 'the universal desolation of your own selves' that they could expect [**doc. 14**]. Morrison in his *Lamentation* painted a vivid picture of the results of sedition; virgins ravished, death, robbery and spoil. He went on to ask how anyone could deliberately reduce the country to such a state. Morrison's treatises were intended to rally the support of the gentry in the crisis of the Henrician Reformation. So he appealed directly to their insecurity in the face of the multitude: 'Howe many gentyllmen for lacke of their ventes shalbe fayn to lay their landes to mortgage?' Morrison saw rebellion in harsh economic terms. Even 'in time of peace be not all men almost at war with them that be rich?' he once wrote. His emphasis in *A Remedy for Sedition* is on the threat to wealth and property 'whan every man wyll rule' (**85,** pp. 200–2). He is here almost Marxist in his analysis [**doc. 10**].

In 1536 and again in 1549 the threat that enemies abroad would use the moment of weakness at home to invade caused the government considerable anxiety. In both cases it became an important argument in their propaganda. 'If Lincolnshire seke to distroye Englande, what wonder is hit if Fraunce and Scotlande sometime have fought to offende me?' asked Morrison. In these passages he appealed directly to the 'men of Lincolnshire' though it was highly unlikely that copies of his books would come into the hands of the rebels themselves. He used the image of the ship of state, familiar in political theory, to drive home his point: 'What folly, what madnes is this, to make an hole in the shyppe that thou saylest in?' Somerset in a letter to the western rebels in 1549 concentrated on warning them of the disastrous consequences of 'your owne foly and sturdines'. The French were rumoured to be preparing an attack on the Scilly Isles: 'Yf they shulde descend and take place wolde not they then rob and spoile pill and subdue you?' He told the Devonshire justices to employ the same argument [**doc. 15**].

Finally the appeal to history was used to show how rebellions had always failed in the past. Archbishop Cranmer provided Old Testament examples in his sermon on rebellion in 1549, describing the fate of the children of Israel who rebelled against Moses. He brought his message home with more immediate cases and maintained that in the slaughter following the failure of the peasants war in Germany, in 1525, over 100,000 rebels were killed in three months. Richard Morrison in his *Lamentation* catalogued the rebels who had failed in the fourteenth and fifteenth centuries. He reminded his readers of the way Henry VII had dealt with the Cornishmen on Blackheath field only thirty-nine years before.

2 Rebellion and the Social Structure

The realities of sixteenth-century life increasingly disturbed the traditional theory of a harmonious and static social order. The flood of monastic, chantry and crown lands produced an open and speculative land market. The growth of the London and provincial food markets (**59**), galloping inflation and increased commercial activity and litigation offered exceptional opportunities for social mobility in Tudor England. This mobility is supported by statistical evidence for the later part of the century and was noted and commented on by contemporaries (**74**). In order to preserve the ideal of a static social structure those who were successful in the competition for social advancement made frenzied efforts to conceal their movement in society by inventing pedigrees or taking arms (**38**). From the 1540s onwards, the government, who disliked and found dangerous a society so full of opportunities, used their control of the pulpit to propagate the homilies of obedience. They recognised that in the last resort the security of their ideal of obedience to the old and the titled lay in the family. So we find Lord Russell in 1549 being urged, in Protector Somerset's orders on the quashing of the Western Rebellion, to give special charge to masters and fathers to have 'an earnest continual regard to the good governance of their children and servants'.

The attitudes and standards which determined the hierarchy of social status that was so important in a Tudor community are subtle and difficult to determine. There was sometimes disagreement when a man died as to whether his new house and prosperous farm had entitled him to move up a rung on the ladder. A man might refer to himself in his will as a yeoman but be called a husbandman by his neighbours who made the inventory of his farm. Boundaries between social groups could become blurred as families struggled to move upwards. But the most important distinction in Tudor society remained that between gentry and commons. To be accepted as a gentleman a man had to be rich enough not to have to work and he had to be able to display the standard of living expected of the gentry.

In the vast majority of cases yeomen families slipped quietly into the ranks of the gentry without disturbing the harmony of kinship and friendship in the village. But where there was serious pressure of population on natural resources, or a gentlemen exploited the opportunities economic conditions offered at the expense of the commons, envy of the rich might quickly turn to open and violent class hostility [**doc. 18**].

The commons of Tudor England, that vast mass of the people who had no political role and could only bring their grievances to the attention of the government by rebellion, were regarded by the gentry as fickle, irrational and stupid (**61**). 'The people', said Archbishop Whitgift, 'are commonly bent to novelties and to factions and most ready to receive that doctrine that seemeth to be contrary to the present state and that inclineth to liberty.' The gentry regarded the multitude as beneath contempt. 'The poorer and meaner people . . . have no interest in the commonwealth but the use of breath', was Sir Thomas Smith's opinion in 1565. Yet as a 'many headed monster' the commons were feared: as the aim of government propaganda in time of rebellion was to ensure the loyalty of the gentry it was usual to emphasise the base origins of the 'rascal mob' and make little of such gentry support as the rebels maintained. Acts of violence against the nobility, such as the killing of Lord Sheffield by Kett's rebels, were useful material to men like Sir John Cheke, employed to paint a picture of traitors who presumed to usurp the political role of their superiors.

The Henrician and Edwardian publicists filled their works with much crude social hostility. But only in the case of the 1549 rebellions, where other sources confirm their accounts, was class hostility a major element in sixteenth-century popular disorder. The tradition of deference survived the upheavals of the century. Even in time of rebellion the fundamental assumptions of Tudor society persisted: the commons expected the gentry to give the lead. If the gentry closed the gates of their parks and retired to their manor houses the commons went and sought them out. They persuaded them, or in some cases in 1497 and 1536 forced them, to take their side. Rebellion needed a gentleman of reputation and personality to have any chance of success; a popular rising planned as part of a wider conspiracy, as was Wyatt's Rebellion in 1554, was potentially the most serious menace a Tudor government might have to face.

The relationship of landlord and tenant was the prime cohesive force of Tudor society. It was a relationship involving responsibilities and obligations on both sides (**82,** p. 294 and 336). It contained a strong moral element. Because the relationships on which village communities rested were personal and intimate the majority of landlords did not exploit their tenants. Sir John Gostwick's memorandum of advice to his heir on estate management, written in 1540, shows his concern to retain his credit as a good landlord and to do well by God and the King. He told his successor not to increase his tenants' rents unless they were imposing increases on their own subtenants (**12,** p. 161).

In the north the close bonds of provincial society took additional strength from the survival until towards the end of the Tudor period of the dominance of such families as the Percies, Cliffords and Dacres whose power, once based on livery and maintenance, continued through appointments in their households, to stewards of their lordships and to constables of their castles. The idea of faithfulness to a magnate connection survived even into the seventeenth century (**65**). In 1619 Sir Henry Curwen, himself sheriff and knight of the shire in Cumberland, 'humbly tendered his service' to the ninth earl of Northumberland from Workington, 'that place wherein many of my ancestors have been servants'. 'My ancestors', he wrote, 'always have been imployed in service in that noble house of Northumberland, and although I acknowledge myself inferior to the meanest of them, yet none of them have ever borne a more faithful affection to that famous house.'

Part Two

DESCRIPTIVE ANALYSIS

3 Taxation and Rebellion

It was an accepted principle in the fifteenth century that the king should only tax his people for the needs of war or in other exceptional circumstances, and through the consent of parliament. In fact an Act of 1483 declared that non-parliamentary taxation was illegal. Parliamentary opposition to taxation concentrated on restricting the total amount granted and the way in which the money should be levied and spent.

The commons' growing distrust of the crown's financial motives is illustrated by their insistence in 1497, following the Treaty of Etaples five years before, that parts of their grants should be dependent on the crown actually undertaking specified military expeditions. In 1523 the opposition to Wolsey's subsidy demands was prolonged and heated. But even then no one, unless Cromwell did actually deliver the speech which survives in the hand of one of his clerks, went so far as to question Henry VIII's grand design against France (**11**, p. 19).

At the local level popular dislike of taxation was expressed in sporadic outbreaks of violence against tax collectors. In the period 1485–1547 there were eleven recorded cases of assaults on tax collectors, concentrated around London and the south coast and there were probably others which never reached the courts. More common and more widely spread geographically are cases of the forcible rescue of goods, distressed by a tax commissioner from a man who had refused to pay; 112 such cases are recorded (**77**). It is against this parliamentary and local background that we must examine the more determined resistance to taxation in this period. Twice, in 1489 and 1497, this amounted to rebellion and was ruthlessly crushed. Twice, in 1513 and 1525, the resistance was passive and succeeded.

THE YORKSHIRE REBELLION 1489

The rebellion in Yorkshire in April 1489 arose from the efforts of the Fourth Earl of Northumberland, who was Lieutenant General of the Middle and Eastern Marches, to collect the subsidy for that year. This had been granted by parliament to enable Henry VII to intervene on behalf of Brittany against the French crown (**45,** p. 35). Northumberland was met by a mob of Yorkshiremen and assassinated at Topcliffe, near Thirsk. The rioting that followed under the leadership of Sir John Egremont caused the king to make plans to lead an army north. But when the Earl of Surrey quickly crushed the rising this became unnecessary.

Although this was a protest against war taxation, the rising contained other strangely diffuse elements. Polydore Vergil and the Great Chronicle of London mention the rebels' sympathy with the Yorkist cause. An incoherent proclamation which survives among the Paston Letters says that the rebels intended 'to geynstonde such persons as is aboutward for to dystroy oure suffereyn Lorde the Kynge and the Commons of Engelond, for suche unlawfull poyntes as Seynt Thomas of Cauntyrbery dyed for'. This evidence that the name of Becket as a man who stood against the King had survived in popular folklore is interesting; the reference is presumably to the Act of 1489 on benefit of clergy (**12,** p. 89). The accounts of the assassination in Skelton's elegy of Northumberland and William Peeris's Percy chronicle emphasise sinister implications of treachery behind it. The Earl was abandoned by his retinue, 'those to whom he gave fees and was right speciall lord', who fled leaving him to the mercy of an assassin who was a royal officer. A recent analysis has suggested that the rising was directed at this powerful provincial magnate rather than the crown (**63**). The minority of the fifth earl, a ward of the crown, then gave Henry VII a useful opportunity to assert royal power in the north against the Percies. The longstanding enmity between Percies and Tudors followed.

THE CORNISH REBELLION 1497

In 1497 it was Cornwall that rebelled. Henry had turned his attention towards Scotland and wanted money to deal with Perkin Warbeck, who had received a ready welcome from James IV

(**19,** p. 86). In all, in one subsidy and two fifteenths and tenths, the country paid the king £88,606 in this year. This was far more than was paid in any other year of the reign. Only in 1492, when £56,311 was paid in taxation, did the yield of parliamentary grants exceed £31,000 (**77**). But the Cornishmen objected to paying taxes for war against Scotland; the whole problem of the north seemed much too remote to them. They were encouraged to resist by an able Bodmin lawyer, Thomas Flamank, who handled arguments about scutage with confidence. According to Bacon, he maintained that

> subsidies were not to be granted, nor levied in this case, that is for wars of Scotland; for that the law had provided another course, by service of escuage for those journeys; much less when all was quiet and war was made but a pretence to poll and pill the people.

The chronicler Edward Hall described Cornwall as a country 'sterile and without all fecundity', where men 'gate their lyvyng hardly by mining and digging tynne and metall oute of the grounde bothe day and night labourying and turmoylyng'. Subsidies, which were being transformed by the early Tudors into a method of raising much larger sums of money than was possible through the traditional fifteenth and tenth, fell hard on the poorer section of the community. It is significant that in 1489 and 1497, and again in 1536, it was a subsidy rather than a fifteenth and tenth that the commons resisted.

Persuaded by Flamank to direct their resentment against the king's evil advisers Cardinal Morton and Sir Reginald Bray, the Cornishmen made a remarkable march across England to present their grievances to the government. They were led by Flamank and Michael Joseph, a blacksmith from the Lizard area. At Taunton, according to Hall, they slew a subsidy commissioner, but otherwise the march was orderly. At Wells they were joined by Lord Audley, an impoverished and discontented nobleman, who, says Polydore Vergil, they 'with acclamation accepted as their chief'.

Henry had been caught unawares; by 13 June the Cornishmen, said to number 15,000, were at Guildford. The army of 8,000 that was being prepared against Scotland under Lord Daubeney had to be rapidly diverted. After a brief encounter between 500 of Daubeney's spearmen and the rebels near Guildford, the Cornishmen continued their march round the south of London. Meanwhile the king himself gathered forces at Henley and on 16th June was able to join Daubeney, who was protecting the approaches to the city. The London chronicler tells how 'the king was seen in the feelde, and abrewyng and comfortyng of his people'. The same day the Cornishmen came up to Blackheath where at last they could look down on London. Many were disillusioned by their failure to attract support in Kent, and lost heart when they found the leaders were preparing for battle. Guns were placed to defend the passage of the river at Deptford. The London chronicler relates how the rebel camp was 'all that night in greate agony and variaunce; ffor some of thym were mynded to have comyn to the Kyng and to have yolded theym and put theym fully in his mercy and grace; but the smith was of the contrary myende'. A large number did desert and only about 10,000 were left to face the army, said to number 25,000, that the king had mustered.

Henry not only concentrated overwhelming forces but planned his attack meticulously, sending a force of archers and cavalry round the back of the rebels. He had only defeated Lambert Simnel at Stoke ten years before after a stiff three hour contest. This time he wanted a quick and crushing victory. After Daubeney had gained the Deptford bridge he was taken prisoner, but released almost at once. Bacon concludes the story: 'The Cornishmen, being ill-armed and ill-led and without horse or artillery, were with no great difficulty cut in pieces and put to flight.' The king entered the city over London bridge and was received by the mayor, 'to whom he gave cherefull thankes for his good diligence of kepyng and orderyng of the Citie . . . and from thens rode unto Powlis and there offred'.

Many of the rebels died on the field. Audley was executed and Flamank and Joseph were hung, drawn and quartered. Henry cancelled an order that their dismembered bodies should be exhibited throughout Cornwall through fear of the rumours that the country was 'still eager to promote a revolution if they were in anyway provoked'. But he proceeded to fine all those involved in the rebellion with systematic severity. He took in all from the Cornishmen, including Warbeck's adherents later in the year, £14,699. 'The less blood he drew', said Bacon of the first Tudor king, 'the more he took of treasure'.

RESISTANCE TO TAXATION 1513–25

It was not until 1513 that people again found themselves expected to pay a subsidy and a fifteenth and tenth in the same year. The total yield of parliamentary taxation levied in this year was £62,126. Polydore Vergil provides the only account of the passive resistance in Yorkshire. He noted that the 'sudden new upheaval of the north country folk' was caused 'by the heaviness of the tax imposed a little earlier'. As in 1497 the burden imposed by the government was exceptional. According to Vergil 'these north country folk volunteered their personal services in waging war, but they refused the money because they have so little of it'. His account is confirmed by evidence that the commissioners for collecting the subsidy in the West Riding wapentakes of Staincliffe and Ewcross had difficulty in making their assessments, which ought to have been returned by early summer (**79, 99,** pp. 198–9). They were not finally returned until 1515 and the towns of Dent and Sedbergh still refused to appear in January of that year. The general poverty of these wapentakes is not in doubt. The king accepted a petition from nineteen towns and villages and remitted entirely their payment of the fifteenth and tenth.

In 1523 Wolsey put before parliament heavier financial demands than the commons had ever faced or envisaged. He wanted £800,000 in order to achieve his master's dream of 'the whole monarchy of Christendom' (**45,** chapter 8). The commons, Hall relates, said 'the sum was impossible to be levied'. They argued with some sense that if such a sum of ready money was taken by the king the economy would collapse: 'Then men must barter clothe for vitaille and bread for cheese and so one thyng for another.' In fact the subsidy, phased over four years and collected at much lower rates than Wolsey intended, yielded £151,215. The major part of this, £136,578, had been collected by the spring of 1525. It was at this moment, when the country had just paid out the largest grant in taxation of the whole period 1485–1543, that Wolsey sent out commissioners to collect the Amicable Grant. He was desperate for money to satisfy the king's urge to grasp the opportunity offered by the defeat of France at Pavia.

A. F. Pollard called the Amicable Grant 'perhaps the most violent financial exaction in English history' (**27,** p. 142). It was a levy of one-sixth on the goods of the laity and one-third on the goods of the clergy. Wolsey's idea was to extend the benevolences which Edward IV had extracted from the wealthy and which, as a London councillor had reminded him, the Act of 1483 had forbidden, to the country as a whole. Commissions to collect the grant were sent out in late March to the greatest noble or cleric of each county. There had been some resistance to the 1523 subsidy in Yorkshire where the commons of Craven and Richmondshire had proved recalcitrant; the south-east, however, had paid in full. But the attitude to the new extra-parliamentary grant was from the first sullen and unwilling.

In some places there was direct refusal to pay. Archbishop Warham reported on 12 April that he found the Kentish clergy 'not inclined to the grant' and that heads of religious houses had answered 'that they cannot contribute as they are required'.

Men who said they simply had not the money may have been honest. At Ely they said they would gladly sell their cattle and goods 'but no man in the country has money to buy or lend'. 'Some who at the first loan were well off, now are not worth a groat when their debts are paid.' At Norwich the wealthy aldermen could offer plate but not money. The Duke of Norfolk explained to Wolsey the plight of the large population of poor men who depended on worsted and strawmaking and were paid weekly (**70**).

In a letter of 5 April Warham gave Wolsey a full account of the arguments and attitudes he had encountered. The whole policy of the French war was now called in question. There was no enthusiasm for continental expeditions. Men regretted the captivity of Francis I, the money that had been spent to no purpose on futile expeditions and the king's ambition to win France: Henry VIII 'hath not one foot of land more in France than his most noble father hadd, which lakked no riches or wisdom to wyne the kingdome of France if he had thought it expedient. . . . And if the King win France, he will be obliged to spend his time and revenues there.' Wolsey was the scapegoat but resentment also fell on Warham. He had been called an old fool behind his back for consenting to the grant, he told Wolsey. Anticlericalism emerged quickly in such a situation: 'Some malicious persons say that it would be better for an old fool like him to take his beads in his hand, than to meddle in temporal business pertaining to war and general undoing of this country.'

The collection of the grant made no progress during April.

Reports from East Anglia, Berkshire, Wiltshire and Kent were equally depressing. On 26 April Wolsey told the London councillors that, on the king's advice, he would demand no fixed sums but such as they would willingly grant. When the rumour of his retreat spread in East Anglia the mood of the people hardened. On 8 May the Earl of Essex reported from Stanstead that he had met with determined resistance. After an assembly of 1,000 persons on the Suffolk border, he had suspended proceedings till he heard the king's pleasure: 'Some fear to be hewn in pieces if they make any grant, and there is great danger of more insurrections.'

The most serious rising was in the Lavenham and Sudbury area of Suffolk. Faced with a band of 4,000 men, the Dukes of Norfolk and Suffolk treated the affair cautiously and leniently [**doc. 1**]. Lavenham had paid a total of £354. 1s 4d in the subsidy payments of 1524 and 1525 but a large proportion of this was contributed by rich clothiers, including the Springe family. The wage-earners there numbered just over half the taxable population yet owned less than three per cent of the property. In 1525 it seems many of these men were out of work so it was impossible for them to answer the king's demand.

Wolsey replied to the duke's report by urging strong measures. When the four 'principal offenders' he had arrested were brought to London however Henry showed his political sense by bowing before the storm. He abandoned the grant. At 'a great counsaill', relates Hall, 'he openly said that his mind was not to ask anything of his commons which might sound to his dishonour or to the breach of his laws'. When the king inquired how the commissioners' demands came to be so strict 'the Cardinal excused himself'. At the end of May the ringleaders were brought before Star Chamber and pardoned after they had been 'shown their offences, with terrible words' (**89,** pp. 51–2; **97,** pp. 135–9).

The resistance to the Amicable Grant made Henry realise that in the last resort his kingship rested on his partnership with the tax-paying classes. He found himself up against the vocally expressed public opinion of south-east England, of the counties on which the strength of Tudor monarchy rested. The affair had begun with propaganda. The commissioners had been told to make solemn processions and bonfires in celebration of the French king's defeat before they began collecting the money. It ended in open retreat. Tudor monarchs always found it needed discussion and concession to obtain taxes from parliament. On this occasion the government found itself proceeding from persuasion to concession in face of extra-parliamentary opinion. It may not be entirely irrelevant that Hall noted in his chronicle for 1525 that 'in this troublous season the uplandish men of Germany rose in a great number, almost an hundred thousand, and rebelled against the princes of Germany'.

Popular opinion had made a significant impact on foreign policy. Henry was forced to abandon his schemes for European hegemony, and peace with France was the only course (**45,** p. 109). When in the 1540s he again became involved in large scale continental commitments, the gentry made large grants of taxation. But, if Henry had not been dispensing monastic lands to attract their loyalty, he might have found the taxpayers unwilling again then. The total yield of parliamentary taxes in the period 1541–7 was £656,245. Even bearing in mind the beginnings of the inflation, this is an astounding figure. In the whole of Henry VII's reign the country had paid only £282,000, and in the period 1509–40 the total came to £520,463. Despite the resistance to taxation that has been discussed in this chapter, the development of the subsidy into a system of assessment and collection of greater complexity than anything before attempted must be rated a spectacular achievement by the early Tudors. The historian of parliamentary taxation in this period has concluded that there was 'a growing concurrence on the part of the taxable population in the aims and interests of the crown' (**77**). The resistance was always highly localised; where it was determined it seems to have been based on real poverty.

4 The Pilgrimage of Grace

THE LINCOLNSHIRE RISING

Three government commissions were at work in Lincolnshire at Michaelmas in 1536. That for dissolving the smaller monasteries had been in the county since June, a second commission was assessing and collecting the subsidy and a third was appointed to enquire into the fitness and education of the clergy. They worked in an atmosphere of rumour and alarm. It was said that jewels and plate were to be confiscated from parish churches, that all gold was to be taken to the mint to be tested, and that taxes were to be levied on all horned cattle, and on christenings, marriages and burials. There were even wilder rumours: 'that there shall be no church within five miles, and that all the rest shall be put down', that men would not be allowed to eat white bread, goose or capon without paying a tribute to the king. It was said that every man would have to give an account of his property and income and a false return would lead to forefeiture of all his goods. There is evidence that these rumours had spread to many parts of the eastern and midland counties by the autumn of 1536. But they were strongest in Lincolnshire. The rising there, based on the three towns of Louth, Caistor and Horncastle, was an outburst by men who, as Wriothesley told Cromwell, 'think they shall be undone for ever' (**89**).

The rising began at Louth, where the people were immensely proud of the magnificent spire of their church completed only twenty years before. When the Bishop of Lincoln's registrar arrived there on 2 October to carry out the visitation of the clergy, he was seized by the commons who had been guarding the treasure house of the church all the night before. They were led by the shoemaker Nicholas Melton, or Captain Cobbler as he came to be called. The commons made the registrar and the assembled priests swear on oath to be true to them and burnt the registrar's papers. Then they marched to Legbourne nunnery and captured the royal commissioners who were at work there.

The Louth outburst was the signal for a rising throughout the county. Captain Cobbler disregarded a message that reached him on 2 October that Yorkshire was not ready to rise and ordered a muster for the next day. On 3 October the commission for the subsidy was due to meet at Caistor. The priests of the neighbourhood were there also to attend the commissary's court. The commons were alarmed by a rumour that their weapons were going to be confiscated and the priests feared their examination. The commissioners hoped to reason with the people but when the commons of Louth, 3,000 strong, came in sight they turned their horses and fled. Several of the commissioners were captured by the commons and agreed to support them. That evening four of them signed a letter to the king requesting a general pardon for the assembly caused by the 'common voice and fame ... of newe enhaunsements and other importunate charges'.

By 4 October the gentry had confidently assumed the leadership of the rising. Their willing involvement gave the movement an air of legitimacy, transforming it from a plebeian riot into a demonstration, constrained throughout by respect for established authority including that of the King, against certain of his policies. (**89**) In north Lincolnshire gentry mobilised their own wapentakes through the machinery of musters; at Horncastle gentlemen appeared at a rebel rally 'well harnassed with their tenants'. No attempt was made to hold back the commons from violence. When Dr Raynes, the hated chancellor of the Bishop of Lincoln, was brought to the Horncastle muster on 4 October the frenzied mob set upon him and murdered him with their staves. It was left to the sheriff to divide his clothes and the money in his purse among the crowd. It was on this occasion that the gentry drew up the first manifesto of the rising. This document like the later articles combined the commons grievances with those of the gentry [**doc. 2**].

At least 10,000 men marched to Lincoln. Since the ancient landed families, who as J.P.s were responsible for order in the shire, had thrown in their lot with the rising there was no one to stop its progress. The parish clergy played a crucial role in mobilising the movement and monks from Barlings, Bardney and Kirkstead joined the rebel host horsed and armed. (**81**) Lord Hussey, the principal nobleman of the county, hoped to mediate between the dissidents and the court, manoeuvred, hesitated and in the end defected (**89,** pp. 52–65).

At Lincoln a new set of articles was drawn up and sent to London. The gentry had difficulty in restraining the commons' impatient demand to proceed to the general muster planned to take place at Ancaster, near Grantham, on 8 October. When the king's reply, threatening extreme punishment if the rebels did not disperse at once, reached Lincoln on 10 October, the royal army under the Duke of Suffolk was already only forty miles away at Stamford. For the eighteen principal gentry involved this was the moment of choice. Any further resistance was treason. They decided to sue for pardon and told the commons they would not go forward. At this there was bitter recrimination against the gentry and the rising dissolved into confusion. When Lancaster Herald arrived at Lincoln on 11 October many had already slipped away. He persuaded the rest to go home.

When the men of Horncastle reached home they placed the banner they had designed for themselves in their church. It showed the Five Wounds of Christ, proclaiming that the commons fought in Christ's cause. The other symbols on the Horncastle banner illustrate the confused purposes of the Lincolnshire rising. A chalice with the host appeared to show the commons' fear that church plate was going to be confiscated, the plough symbolised the impact of enclosure for pasture on the husbandman, and a horn may have stood for their town or the rumoured tax on horned cattle.

The rebellion collapsed quickly because it lacked a determined popular leader. Captain Cobbler remains a shadowy figure. 'The commons did nothing but by the gentlemen's commandment, and they durst never stir in the field from the place they were appointed to till the gentlemen directed them what to do', said a witness. The Louth commissioners were unwilling from the start and acted on the commons' behalf through fear. But the Horncastle gentry were much less reluctant. If the deposition of the priest Nicholas Leache, who was with the Horncastle company, can be trusted, the Dymnokes took the lead in 'harnessing' themselves, as well as in drawing up the first set of articles [**doc. 2**]. The momentum of the rising always depended on the gentry, and when they turned back its uncertainty and hollowness was revealed. For ten days gentry and commons worked in an uneasy partnership, as their interests were widely separated. Hatred of the unpopular Bishop of Lincoln and an unpopular tax held the commons together, but they could only express themselves in brutal and sordid behaviour: the Horncastle murder overlay such idealism as the rising possessed. Lincolnshire's attempt to reverse the Henrician Reformation must be assessed as chaotic and feeble.

THE PILGRIMAGE: OCTOBER–DECEMBER 1536

On 4 October 1536 Robert Aske, beginning his return journey to London for the law term, crossed the Humber at Barton and heard from the ferryman about the Lincolnshire rising. Later that day he took the rebels oath. Aske was an astute and successful lawyer: he held a number of grievances against the Cromwellian regime. But when, two days later, he found the men of Marshland and Howdenshire on the point of ringing their church bells to raise the country he tried at first to restrain them, hoping the king might make concessions to the Lincolnshire petition. Beverley rose on 8 October when a letter arrived in his name bidding every man to swear to be true to God, the king and the commonwealth, and to maintain the Holy Church. Aske later, in an attempt to exculpate himself, maintained this was forged. But within two days he had taken authority as chief captain and organised the daily musters, the formation of the commons into companies and the appointment of captains in Marshland and Axholme. Other local gentry followed his lead.

On 13 October the companies from the East Riding and Marshland joined up on their march to York. Three days later, already possibly 10,000 strong, they entered the city where the commons had declared for them several days before. It seems to have been during the advance to York that Aske began to speak of the rising as a pilgrimage, telling two messengers 'they were pilgrims and had a pilgrimage gate to go'. His idealistic conception of the rising emerged fully in his second proclamation made at the summons to York:

> For thys pylgrymage we have taken hyt for the preservacyon of Crystes churche, of thys realme of England, the kynge our soverayne lord, the nobylytie and comyns of the same, and to the entent to macke petycion to the kynges highnes for the reformacyon of that whyche is amysse within thys hys realme.

Aske emphasised the Pilgrims' peaceful intentions, saying they meant no 'malys dysplesure to noo persons but suche as be not worthy to remayne nyghe abowte the kynge oure soverayne lordes personne'; yet he maintained also their determination to 'fyght and dye agaynst all those that shalbe abowte towardes to stope us'.

When the mayor yielded, Aske sent him a copy of the Pilgrims' Articles [**doc. 3**]. Their programme at this stage was substantially

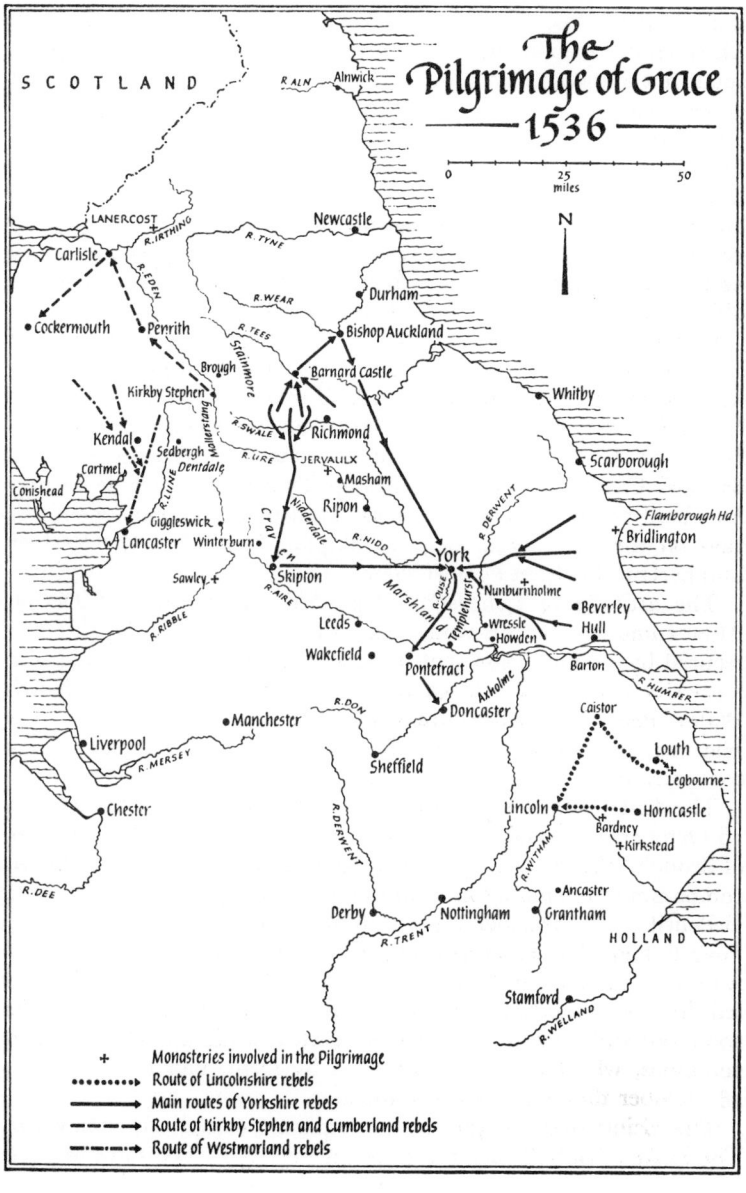

The Pilgrimage of Grace
—1536—

SCOTLAND

LANERCOST
Carlisle
Cockermouth • Penrith
Kirkby Stephen
Brough
Kendal
Cartmel
Sedbergh Dentdale
Conishead
Giggleswick
Lancaster Winterburn
Sawley
Skipton
Leeds
Wakefield •
Manchester
Liverpool
Chester
Sheffield

Alnwick
Newcastle
N
Durham
Bishop Auckland
Barnard Castle
Whitby
Richmond
JERVAULX
Masham
Scarborough
Ripon
Flamborough Hd.
Bridlington
York
Marshland
Nunburnholme
Templehurst
Beverley
Wressle
Hull
Howden
Barton
Pontefract
Axholme
Doncaster
Caistor
Louth
Legbourne
Lincoln
Horncastle
Bardney
Kirkstead
Ancaster
Derby
Nottingham
Grantham
HOLLAND
Stamford

R. ALN
R. TYNE
R. WEAR
R. TEES
Stainmore
R. SWALE
Mallerstang
R. URE
R. LUNE
R. NIDD
R. DERWENT
CRAVEN
Nidderdale
R. AIRE
R. RIBBLE
R. DON
R. MERSEY
R. DERWENT
R. DEE
R. OUSE
R. HUMBER
R. WITHAM
R. TRENT
R. WELLAND
R. IRTHING
R. EDEN

0   25   50
         miles

+   Monasteries involved in the Pilgrimage
•••••••▶ Route of Lincolnshire rebels
————▶   Main routes of Yorkshire rebels
— — —▶   Route of Kirkby Stephen and Cumberland rebels
—·—·—▶   Route of Westmorland rebels

that of the Lincolnshire rebels whose articles had circulated in Marshland. Once in the city Aske took careful precautions against spoil, not allowing any footmen within the walls. He ensured that goods obtained were paid for. He posted on the door of the Minster a plan agreed by the captains for the restoration of religious houses. Only one York house had in fact been effectively suppressed at this time. The nunnery of St Clement's had been dissolved in July 1536 and the nuns were reinstated by the Pilgrims. The government had granted a lease of Holy Trinity Priory in July 1536 but the priory had resisted suppression. The Prior supported the Pilgrimage and did not finally give in until December 1538 (**96,** pp. 10–11).

During the same week that the East Riding rose there were risings in Northumberland and Durham. Richmondshire, Mashamshire, Sedbergh and Nidderdale also all rose about 11 October. The North Riding company swore in Lord Latimer and Sir Christopher Danby as their leaders and went north to force the surrender of Barnard Castle. They spoiled Bishop Tunstall's palace at Bishop Auckland before marching to York. Half their company spent ten days on the way laying siege to Skipton Castle but the Earl of Cumberland held out against them.

The attitude of Lancashire depended on the Earl of Derby. After rumours that he would join the rebellion, his loyalty was secured by a commission sent by Henry on 19 October, giving him authority over a large area of Lancashire, Cheshire and North Wales. People in Lancashire expressed open sympathy with the pilgrims; but, rather than sending a company to join Aske, they concentrated on restoring the abbey of Sawley (**86; 99,** p. 175).

The first musters in Cumberland were at Kirkby Stephen, on 16 October, in response to a summons from Richmond. The vicar of Brough, Robert Thompson, emerged as the local leader and soon companies were coming in from the surrounding villages to musters at Penrith. Here the four captains took the names of Charity, Faith, Poverty and Pity. The rebels hoped to starve out Carlisle and force it to surrender, as Hull had done on 20 October. But Lord Clifford led the town's resistance with determination and on 27 October the commons withdrew to Cockermouth. Meanwhile the Westmorland commons, who had been summoned by Dent, had risen, and on 28 October they marched to Lancaster.

The rising had caught the government completely unawares. The Duke of Suffolk was too busy quietening Lincolnshire to cope with Yorkshire and the Earl of Shrewsbury still awaited the king's orders with his forces at Nottingham. Meanwhile Lord Darcy in Pontefract Castle, known as 'the key to the north', did nothing. He wrote long and desperate appeals to Henry. The castle, he reported on 13 October, had 'not one gun in it ready to shoot' and was 'much out of frame'. Four days later he found himself cut off from the town, which had risen in sympathy with the Pilgrimage. For three weeks the rising was allowed to proceed unimpeded. Only three towns east of the Pennines—Skipton, Scarborough and Newcastle—held out against its surging progress.

Aske's intention throughout the campaign he directed was to overawe the government into granting the demands of the north, by presenting a show of force. He did everything possible to avoid the use of force. Only one man was killed during the Pilgrimage. He did not want to advance south unless Henry refused the Pilgrims' petition and he had no plan to form an alternative government or remove the king. Aske merely wanted to give the north a say in the affairs of the nation, to remove Cromwell and reverse certain policies of the Henrician Reformation. He knew that to make a decisive impact on Henry it was essential to have the backing of the great men of the north. By 19 October he knew also that the whole country beyond the Don was behind him. That day he appeared before Lord Darcy, Edward Lee, the Archbishop of York, and forty or so knights and gentlemen who had taken refuge with Darcy at Pontefract Castle. Aske explained to them the Pilgrims' cause, boldly blaming them for not advising the king of the spread of heresy and the abuses of the monastic visitors. He argued, on practical grounds, that the abbeys should stand, maintaining that they were essential to the economy of the north [**doc. 5**]. He told the archbishop he expected him to mediate for the pilgrims. Two days later Darcy surrendered the castle after threats that the pilgrims would kill his grandchildren.

The archbishop refused to have any part in the Pilgrimage; but the rest of the Pontefract gentry now joined in the discussions as to the strategy to be pursued against the approaching royal army. Darcy and Sir Robert Constable quickly became leaders among the rebels. On the day the castle had surrendered the king had sent Shrewsbury orders to advance and hold the Don. This he did. Meanwhile the Duke of Norfolk, who Henry had appointed to command the royal army, sent a message to the pilgrims by

Lancaster Herald. Norfolk suggested that bloodshed might be avoided if four of the pilgrims came to Doncaster to explain the causes of their rising.

There was disagreement among the pilgrims as to whether they should treat with Norfolk. Their army of 30,000 was well disciplined and overwhelmingly strong beside the 8,000 men at the most that Shrewsbury had with him across the Don. But Aske argued that Norfolk, remembered and respected in the north as a hero of Flodden, might use his influence at court on their behalf. He wanted to trust Norfolk and he won. Those who doubted Norfolk's intentions were more realistic, as before the meeting on Doncaster Bridge he wrote to Henry: 'I beseech you to take in gode part what so ever promes I shall make unto the rebells for sewerly I shall observe no part thereoff.'

The leaders decided to make their petition to Norfolk very general, leaving the maximum room for negotiation. Their five articles were in substance those drawn up before York; but instead of mentioning the acts for the subsidy and the supression and the Statute of Uses by name they merely asked that 'unpopular statutes might be repealed' and 'the Faith truly maintained' (**83**), [**doc. 3**]. Aske did not go to the bridge himself but ordered a general muster of the pilgrims on the plain beyond it. This was the climax of the northern demonstration. But the bond between gentry and commons was still fragile. Some murmured that the gentlemen would betray them as they waited the return of the lords and knights.

No full account of the meeting on 27 October survives but, from a conversation between Darcy and Somerset Herald a few weeks later, it appears that Norfolk did his utmost to bring the gentry to treachery. It is easy to dismiss Lord Darcy, an old man of almost eighty, as a reactionary trying to hold up the tide of Henrician centralisation yet his brand of old fashioned chivalry deserves respect (**11**).

> I had rather have my hed stryken of [he told the herald], than I wold defyle my cote armor, for it shall never be sayd that old Thome shall have one treators tothe in his hed. . . . For my part I have byn and ever wylbe true both to kyng henry the vii and to the kyng our soverayn lord and I defye hym that wyll say the contrary, for as I have ever say one god one feth and one kyng.

But when it came to giving up his captain whose cause was the unity of the commonwealth he could not do it:

For he that promysseth to be true to one, and deseyveth him, may be called a treator: whych shall never be seyd in me for what is a man but is promysse.

Here is the central dilemma of the pilgrim leaders, a dilemma that faced Aske when in his examination he was asked how he could reconcile his duty of obedience to the king with the oath he swore on 4 October. It was a dilemma that neither Darcy, Aske, nor any of the pilgrims, could solve.

Attractive as Darcy's idealism may be it was reasoning after the event. There were much more pressing reasons to act as he did and refuse to betray his captain on Doncaster Bridge. He had come to be afraid of his own men who, he told the herald, 'bycause wee tarried a whyll abowght the entreatie wold have ronned apon us to have kylled us sayng that we wold bytray them'. Even more he feared to go to London. 'Hold up thy longe clee and promyse me that I shall have the Kynges favor and shalbe indeferently hard, and I wyll come to Dancastre to yow', he told Shrewsbury. 'Than ye shall not come it' the Earl replied. Darcy knew he had committed himself too far.

The agreement reached on 27 October was that two gentlemen, Sir Ralph Ellerker and Robert Bowes, should carry the pilgrims' petition to the king and a truce should be observed until they returned. Norfolk failed to detach the gentry from the commons so he compromised. He had no choice. It was 'not possible', he reported to the Council, 'to have yeven batayle but upon apparaunt los theroff'. He had 'no horsemen and they all the floure of the north' and most of his own soldiers 'thought and think their quarelles to be gode and godly'.

Ellerker and Bowes reached Windsor on 2 November. The same day the king, in his own hand, wrote a reply to the rebel petition. It was a long justification of his rule emphasising his 'good discretion' in choosing councillors and reproving the pilgrims for rising 'upon false reports and surmises'. One passage displays Henry's characteristic selfrighteous indignation:

What King hath kept you all his subjects so long in wealth and peace . . . so indifferently minister justice to all, both high and low; so defended you all from outward enemies; so fortified the frontiers of this realm, to his no little and in a manner inestimable charges? and all for your wealths and sureties.

Finally he declared his intention through the 'pity and compassion' of 'our princely heart' to pardon all but ten ringleaders.

Henry thought that the rebellion would now collapse as it had done in Lincolnshire. His paramount concern was to claim victims and display his victory. He can be credited with the political sense to see that at this crisis of his reign it was essential to preserve face and maintain unbroken the prestige of Tudor monarchy. He knew he could not afford to make concessions to this challenge as he had to the passive resistance of 1525. Nevertheless his blustering self-confidence was misplaced. Norfolk realised that the best policy was to temporise and so he persuaded the king to delay proclaiming his reply in the north. When Ellerker and Bowes laid the king's message before the chief captains of the Pilgrimage at Darcy's home at Templehurst on 18 November, it contained no reply to the articles but an offer of further negotiations between 300 of the pilgrims, under safe conduct if they wished, and the Duke of Norfolk.

Henry's original reply had in fact been released and read at Skipton a few days before. It had increased the already extreme uneasiness of the truce. The movements of royal troops, particularly just south of the Humber, and rumours of a siege of Hull and a plot to capture Aske, alarmed the north throughout the first fortnight of November. The delay in the return of Ellerker and Bowes was regarded with the utmost suspicion. Aske and the gentry found it difficult to preserve the patience of the commons and there were continual complaints on both sides of threatening moves and breaches of the truce.

On 21 November the council of the pilgrims met at York and Robert Bowes gave the captains a detailed account of his visit to Windsor, assuring them that he was satisfied of the king's good faith and mercy. In the discussions which followed one group, led by Sir Robert Constable, were moved by such violent hatred of Cromwell and such fear of his influence over the king that they wanted to 'have all the country made sure from the Trent northwards' and then 'condescend to a meeting'. The rest wanted the conference. It was Constable who read to the council a letter, dated 10 November, from Cromwell to Sir Ralph Evers, who had stood siege through October at Scarborough. If the rebellion continued, Cromwell had said, it would be crushed that 'their example shall be fearful to all subjects whiles the world doth endure'. Despite this glimpse of the government's deviousness, the peace party's argument prevailed.

Nothing, they maintained, could be lost by treating with Norfolk, whose influence it was hoped might rise as Cromwell's waned. Messages were sent to all the counties of the north summoning the pilgrims' representatives to the second meeting at Doncaster.

In his message to the rebels, discussed at York, Henry told them that he found their articles 'general, dark and obscure'. The purpose of the council held at Pontefract from 2 to 4 December was to clarify the issues which the pilgrims should debate at Doncaster and to draw up a definitive statement of their programme. This manifesto was written out by Aske in consultation with Darcy. Each item was then approved by the pilgrim captains. Aske was genuinely concerned to gather the views of all parts of the north. His notices of the Pontefract meeting brought in representatives from all the northern counties. In the final document he was able to combine articles based on the petitions of the commons with the grievances of the gentry as expressed in the statements that several of them drew up. An assembly of north country divines also sat concurrently with the council and made resolutions in sympathy with their programme. Aske regarded it as of the greatest importance that the pilgrims should have the sanction of the church for the stand they had taken. Archbishop Lee was allowed to preach in the parish church on Sunday 3 December in the hope that he would support their cause. But when he told a crowded congregation of gentry and commons that the sword was given to none but a prince the commons exploded in fury. Lee's rebuff was a nasty jolt to the rebels confidence.

Until almost the last moment Henry insisted that Norfolk must except the ringleaders from the pardon; his final instructions, sent on 3 December, were that the duke should grant a general pardon, prolong the truce and promise a parliament wherever the rebels wished it. Norfolk received these orders just before the ten knights, ten esquires, and twenty commons appointed came to him at the White Friars in Doncaster on 6 December. Aske and his companions fell to their knees to beg the king's pardon and favour. Norfolk said that he would grant this and a free parliament. This put him in a strong position when it came to discussing the articles. He was able to argue that most of the acts the pilgrims objected to could be considered at that parliament. He avoided committing himself as to when and where the parliament should be held. On one point the rebels were adamant: the suppressed abbeys should stand until their case had been brought before parliament again. Norfolk had no power to grant this but saw that it was essential if a settlement was to be reached. He compromised by insisting that the abbeys should make a formal surrender to the king's commissioners but that they should then be restored again by the king's authority until the parliament met.

The next morning Aske announced the terms for peace to the 3,000 commons waiting at Pontefract. He was back at Doncaster when he heard that they were not satisfied and threatening to raise all Yorkshire again. He had to return to Pontefract to persuade them that all would be well. When Lancaster Herald had read the king's pardon on 8 December the commons began to go home. The gentlemen meanwhile rode to Doncaster once more and there, in the presence of Norfolk, Aske knelt down and humbly asked the assembly that they should no longer call him captain. They agreed and the pilgrims tore off their badges of the Five Wounds saying: 'We will all wear no badge nor sign but the badge of our sovereign lord.'

Aske thought he had won. Everyone in the north expected Norfolk's speedy return with the king's confirmation of the terms agreed. But for several weeks nothing happened. The king neither ratified nor repudiated the terms that had been made. His policy throughout had been marked by vacillation and inconsistency but now he could await the excuse to exact his revenge and vindicate the honour of his house in bloodshed. The terms had never been written down and Henry no more intended to keep his own promise of a general pardon than Norfolk's that the suppression should be reversed. In London it was rumoured that the rebels had submitted to mercy and the king, his new queen and the court celebrated Christmas with lavishness and splendour. In fact Henry had won (**97**, pp. 341–6).

THE MOTIVES OF THE PILGRIMS

The Pilgrimage of Grace was dominated by the personality of Robert Aske and the historian of the rising cannot escape his magnetism. His lengthy confessions provide the most detailed account of the rebellion (**49**), [**docs 5, 11**]. Aske saw the rising as a religious crusade. He created, in place of the sordidness and confusion of the Lincolnshire rising, a demonstration that had an atmosphere of honour and chivalry. For a few weeks his vision and purposefulness overlaid the divergent interests of gentry and commons with an almost mystical aura. This was a remarkable achievement. But ever since it has been easy for historians of the pilgrimage to see it through the eyes of the chief captain. Aske's idealism cannot be read into the mind of every rebel. M. H. and R. Dodds seriously romanticised the rising (**13**). Professor Dickens in recent assessments has tried to correct the balance (**10, 11, 12**).

Beside the considerable evidence as to Aske's motives, documentation of the attitudes and opinions of the gentry is fragmentary; of the motives of the commons we have virtually no firm evidence at all. The complexity of the interests that the Pilgrimage represented is very clear from the Pontefract manifesto [**doc. 10**]. In many cases the source of particular demands can be established; it is much more difficult to assess the body of opinion each demand represented. We are often forced back on Aske's account to answer questions about the interests of the commons. Aske's confessions are sufficiently corroborated by other evidence for them to be acceptable as the truth so far as he could remember it. By April and May 1537, when he wrote them, he was at the King's mercy and had nothing to gain or lose. Moreover he was quite honest in regard to the articles about which he felt strongly but the commons or other gentry did not. That most of the pilgrims were less altruistic than he, and that their concerns were more mundane cannot be doubted. Nor can it be doubted that the badge of the Five Wounds carried tremendous emotional significance. Who is to say how many of the pilgrims marched because they believed the Church and their faith to be in danger?

The Act for the suppression of the smaller monasteries was passed in March 1536 (**14**). By the summer the suppression commissioners were at work in the north. When they began to carry away the treasures of the Lincolnshire and Yorkshire houses and pension off the religious the impact of the Henrician Reformation was brought home to the commons. The Lincolnshire rising was caused by the wild rumours that spread in the wake of the commissioners. Aske said that men expected the suppression to be 'the distruccion of the holl religeon in Ingland' but he denied that the more fantastic rumours played much part in the Yorkshire rising. If this was so it was because he was so successful in exalting the cause of the monasteries themselves into the rallying cry of the movement.

He emphasised the issue in the York articles [**doc. 3**] and organised the restoration of St Clement's Priory in York. Others like Sir Thomas Percy, however secular their motives in fact, saw the value of religious propaganda. He insisted that the abbot of St Mary's should carry his finest cross at the head of the procession Percy led through York. He sent round the Yorkshire abbeys 'to move the abbots or prior and two monks of every of those houses with the best cross to come forwards in their best array'. Aske disagreed with this policy: he preferred to collect benevolences from the religious to pay his soldiers than to see the monks join the Pilgrimage to fight their own cause.

The reasons why men rose in support of the abbeys ranged from altruism to self interest. The case Aske put forward so ably under examination probably includes most of the motives which made the abbeys, as Norfolk wrote in 1537, 'greatlie beloved with the people' [**doc. 11**]. It is interesting to compare this with the much less sentimental case he argued to the lords at Pontefract [**doc. 5**]. Aske then emphasised the social and economic role of the monasteries. There is no doubt that the day-to-day gifts of food and clothing and hospitality to northern travellers that the houses in the Pennines offered made them valuable to the community as a whole. Their importance to the laity was by no means limited to the three per cent of their income allowable in the Valor Ecclesiasticus as charity [**16**, p. 264). It was the usefulness of the abbeys to the gentry and substantial tenantry that Aske was particularly concerned to emphasise to his Pontefract audience. They acted as the focal point of the social life of a neighbourhood: abbeys provided some rudimentary education, safe deposit for valuable documents, tenancies for farmers, and a place to dispose of unmarried daughters or, through the system of corrodies, aged relations. Aske persuasively maintained that not only would all these services be lost, but that the future economic effects of the appropriation by southern landowners of northern monastic lands would be disastrous. Though exaggerated, his argument that shortage of coin could drive the north into either rebellion or treaty with the Scots was probably not without foundation (**86,** pp. 53–60).

Aske saw the religious role of the monasteries as twofold: they maintained by their 'gostly liffing' an exalted ideal that was to him an essential element of the Christian tradition and they provided 'speritual informacion, and preching' to a people 'not well taught the law of God'. The extent to which the monastic ideal was in fact being realised at the dissolution has been argued over at length by historians. Professor Knowles has now provided a comprehensive and balanced survey of the evidence and dealt with the grosser calumnies of the monastic visitors (**16**). What we are here concerned with is how people other than Aske himself regarded the monasteries in 1536. The pilgrims' ballad makes it evident that the commons did not see their value in definitively religious or economic terms [**doc. 6**]. They lacked the skill and legal training to marshal coherent arguments. They simply identified the threat to the Church with the threat to the poor. In the same way an anonymous petitioner to Aske linked the relief of poverty and 'the prayer for the founders and service of God maintained' (**83,** p. 67).

A review of the course of the pilgrimage supports Aske's claim that, for whatever motives, the suppression was the 'greatest cause' of the rebellion. It appeared in every set of articles from Horncastle to Pontefract [**docs 2, 3, 9**). There is adequately conclusive evidence that at least sixteen of the fifty-five suppressed religious houses of the north were to some extent reoccupied by monks and nuns during the rising. These houses were widely spread through the north from Lanercost in Cumberland to Cartmel and Conishead in Lancashire and Nunburnholme in the East Riding (**86,** pp. 53, 62). It is difficult to determine who took the initiative in these restorations. Aske maintained that St Clement's York was restored 'because the commons would needs put them in'. William Hungate, the farmer of Nunburnholme, held the local inhabitants responsible; there may also have been initiative by the commons behind the restoration of Sawley in Lancashire. That parish priests, monks and friars played an important part in instigating and leading the Pilgrimage is not in doubt. Thomas Maunsell, vicar of Brayton, for example was a ringleader in south Yorkshire (**83,** pp. 64–9; **86; 99,** pp. 179–84).

Perhaps the strongest evidence that the restoration of the abbeys was something that the more vocal commons really cared about is the record of their attitude after the second Doncaster meeting. Norfolk had recognised the determination of the pilgrims on this point yet the compromise he suggested did not leave the commons satisfied. They 'reasoned much for abbeys', says Aske, 'and specially for the possession thereof to the parliament tyme of the Kinges fermers'. It took all Aske's powers of argument to convince them that the religious would be able to return.

The first article at Pontefract, a list of heresies drawn up from books laid before the council, reflects the genuine but theologically uninformed conservatism of the north [**doc. 9**]. Professor Dickens found that the new continental movements had made very little impact on the lower levels of northern society by 1536 (**10**). Henry was fully in sympathy with this demand; he had just had the Ten Articles drawn up in an attempt to end the dangerous 'diversity of opinion'. The rebels were confused as to who the heretics were. At Louth they had burnt copies of the works of John Frith and the New Testament in English. The York list lumps together protestants like Nicholas Shaxton of Salisbury with the orthodox Henrician catholic Longland of Lincoln, who was particularly hated for his administrative policies. Aske admitted that the attack on the 'heretic' bishops reached a prominent position in the final manifesto because it had been in the Lincolnshire petition. It was based on hearsay and vague rumour but it fulfilled the need to find scapegoats. Many people, said Aske, blamed the bishops for 'division in preaching and variance in the Church of England'.

It was the abolition of time-honoured rituals such as the announcement and recognition of holy days, that caused the popular insecurity behind the heresy article. In the East Riding the commons grumbled that they were not allowed to keep St Wilfrid's day. At Kirby Stephen there was fury when the priest failed to bid St Luke's day; at Kendal on the Sunday after Christmas some of the rebels 'stirred up suddenly at beads bidding and would have had the priest bid the beads the old way and pray for the Pope'. A month later they forced the curate to observe these traditional rituals.

The Henrician attack on saint worship also angered the north. The Durham contingent brought with them the banner of St Cuthbert from their cathedral. The badges of the Five Wounds, which Lord Darcy had previously used for his men in an expedition of 1511 against the Moors in Spain, enhanced the idea of a crusade to protect the church 'now lame and fast in boundes' [**doc. 6**]. Yet the commons as a whole did not grasp the more abstruse points which were put forward in the ecclesiastical articles at Pontefract, on the initiative of Aske and a clerical pressure group (articles 2, 5, 18 and 19). The council of divines that had met there gave considerable attention to the 'privalages and rights of the church' and article 18 covers the substance of a number of their resolutions.

The supremacy article was included on Aske's initiative; the same is very likely true of the objection to first fruits and tenths. The divines argued about the Act of Supremacy for some time before agreeing that the king might hold the title of supreme head 'but not exercise any jurisdiction such as visitation'. It may be that only Aske himself and a few others saw an overriding principle at stake: that the supremacy 'could not stand with Goddes law'. Only two of the rebels sent in written petitions on the supremacy issue; yet it would be dangerous to assume from this that it was only Sir Thomas More, Robert Aske and one or two others who really believed that Henry and Cromwell had broken bonds with Rome that mattered. Aske claimed that it was 'in al menz mouthes that the Supremacy should sound to be a measure of a division from the unite of the catholyke church'. Attacks by the clergy on the supremacy and murmuring among the commons are documented in the state papers for these years and were widespread geographically (**58,** p. 34). The 1534 treason Act brought these attacks on the King within the law. 394 people in all were tried for treason by words in the years 1532–40, many of them because they had been heard to express objections to the Supremacy (**85,** pp. 263–92, 387). Article 21 specifically attacked 'treasons for wordes'.

Dislike of taxation was as persistent a theme in the rebel articles as the suppression of the monasteries [**docs 2, 3, 9**]. The risings in the Yorkshire dales and Marshland seem to have been partly due to the government's financial demands: the evidence of tax assessments in the early Tudor period has shown that these were the poorest areas of the West Riding (**79; 85,** p. 29). The taxes came after two years of dearth following bad weather and harvests. Besides Cromwell's subsidy and fifteenth had a certain novelty, in that they attempted to extend the king's right of parliamentary taxation into times of peace. R. S. Schofield sees the subsidy act of 1534 as revolutionary in that it 'justifies parliamentary taxation primarily in terms of the civil benefits conferred on the realm by the excellence of the king's government' (**77**). This point was not missed in the north. When Holland rose to support the rest of Lincolnshire their articles stated that the king should demand no more money of his subjects except for the defence of the realm.

The violent resistance of the north to the 1534 taxation Acts was in fact quite irrational. Only about 1·4 per cent of the population normally liable to be taxed were actually being assessed. And the yield of the fifteenth and two subsidies levied by parliament in this decade was only £80,384, a small total compared with the two previous decades. The resistance must therefore be seen in the context of the general suspicion and fear of the intentions of the crown (**83**). The outlook of the commons was political as well as economic. It consisted of a deeply felt resentment at southern interference with the northern way of life [**doc. 9,** articles 4, 8, 10, 11, 14 and 19]. Cromwell was the principal scapegoat: he was 'in such horror and hatred of the people in those parts', said Aske, 'that in manner they would eat him and esteem their griefs only to arise by him and his counsel' [**doc. 8**]. The gentry detested him for trying the Yorkshire grand jury in Star Chamber for wrongfully acquitting a murderer. Exaggerated stories circulated about the bribery and spoliation of the unscrupulous monastic visitors Doctors Legh and Layton, who had been at York, Richmond and Whitby, among other houses, in February 1536. Archbishop Cranmer and Richard Rich, the Chancellor of the Court of Augmentations set up to manage the monastic lands, were disliked because they were identified with the radical party in Church and state. The pilgrims' ballad popularised the victimisation of these accomplices of Cromwell [**doc. 6**].

The Pilgrimage must be seen therefore as a united attack by the gentry and commons of the north on the Cromwellian regime as a whole. Henry in his reply to the rebels' petition maintained that there were now more noblemen in his council than at the beginning of his reign. The attitude of his official propagandist contrasts sharply with the king's evasion of the issue. The crisis of 1536 gave Richard Morrison the opportunity to write the first open justification of the ideal of educational opportunity, a society open to talents, to which he and his party aspired (**48**). 'A waye muste be founde that they rule that beste can': this was Morrison's argument [**doc. 10**]. He answered the challenge of the socially conservative north by an appeal to the claims of virtue over birth. Thus we find the defenders of order using a theory of democratic advancement that required careful expression if it was not to contradict the Great Chain of Being. Who were those who should rule? Morrison, in his first draft of *A Remedy for Sedition*, wrote that 'those that nature hathe either indewd with greater giftes or fortune sette in higher degree tha other' should have authority to govern. It is interesting to see how he qualified this in his final version [**doc. 10**].

If the indiscriminate particularism of the northern commons was an important element in the rising, the political content of a number of the articles in Pontefract manifesto was nevertheless the work of a small group of gentry. The process by which the gentry imposed their own grievances on the Lincolnshire rising was clearly described by Nicholas Leche [**docs. 2, 3,** article 2, and **doc. 9,** article 20). They were most concerned about the Statute of Uses, which appears in all the rebel manifestoes (**83; 80**). There may have been some genuine popular feeling for Princess Mary, as Aske claimed, but he himself was probably responsible for the demand that she should be legitmised (article 3). As usual his arguments were both theoretical and practical. He emphasised his doubts as to the legality of the divorce, recalled that 'on the mother syd she was comyn of the greatest blood and paraige of Cristyndome'; he also expressed his fear that if she was not favoured 'the emperour and his frendes should thinke he had cause therby to move ware agenst this realme and stop the recours of our merchandise into Flanders'.

The article about Mary should be seen in the context of the general dissatisfaction of Aske and his friends at Henry's decision that he would will the crown as he desired, now embodied in an Act of parliament [**doc. 9,** article 16]. This left the question of Henry's successor in considerable confusion and the northern gentry in a state of unhappy insecurity. Among the commons there were absurd rumours that Cromwell might be brought into the succession. Aske's fears were more realistic: unless it was definitely established that Mary should succeed, the king might look seriously at the Scottish claim, through his sister Margaret. Aske was determined that 'if the crown were given by the King's highness to an alien . . . it is a void gift, because he is not born under the allegiance of this crown'.

The complaint against abuses of the common law, the demand for judicial decentralisation and for more control of extortion by escheators, to be repeated in Norfolk in 1549, all reflect the thinking of Aske himself (articles 22, 23 and 24). The two Pontefract articles on parliament (articles 12 and 15) however, were included by Aske after he had read an important paper by Sir Thomas Tempest, who had sat as member for Newcastle-on-Tyne from 1529–36 [**doc. 8**]. They also reflect the political attitudes of Lord Darcy. Darcy and Tempest felt strongly about the way parliament had been muzzled and controlled by Cromwell. Darcy had disapproved of royal policies since 1529 and in 1532 openly opposed Norfolk in the debate on matrimonial causes, speaking his mind on the divorce. In January 1534 he had been informed that his presence in the Lords was no longer required and later that year he began secret treasonable discussions with Chapuys. Darcy, as a leader of the opposition party in the House of Lords, had not failed to notice the small changes in procedure that helped the government to proceed with the programme of the Henrician Reformation. It had been usual to send the lords a copy of all Bills on matters touching the prerogative; then they were told 'that they could have no such copy upon their suyt'. Darcy also 'thought defaut in tho of the Chauncery, in the usse of ther office emonges the lordes, and in the hastie reding of the billes and request of the sped of the same' (**93,** pp. 254–5).

Sir Thomas Tempest clearly regarded the Cromwellian parliament as a mere puppet of the king's minister [**doc. 8**]. His petition is a forthright and thoughtfully argued exposition of the responsibilities of kingship. He vigorously attacked the system of appointment of placemen, of whom he instanced Sir Francis Brian. In his petition and in some propositions attributed to Aske we have some evidence that Cromwell's painstakingly efficient management of parliament was not without repercussions (**14**). Aske said that burgesses should be residents of the boroughs they represented. He pointed out that 'the old custom that none of the King's servants should be of the Commons House' was not observed. There was also dissatisfaction at the under-representation of the north. Only York, Hull and Scarborough were represented in 1529; at Doncaster it was suggested that Beverley, Ripon, Richmond, Pontefract, Wakefield, Skipton and Kendal should all send burgesses to the Commons.

Before examining the social and economic grievances of the north, it is necessary to say something of the great magnate families beyond the Trent. The structure of northern society was founded on the vast networks of influence and patronage that these families exercised. Two of the nobility were central figures in the crisis of 1536: Henry Percy was sixth Earl of Northumberland and Henry Clifford was first Earl of Cumberland. Their attitudes and behaviour when the tensions of the north burst into rebellion were governed by their local standing and their relationships with the crown. The courses they followed sharply diverged and brought them, despite a close tie by marriage, into bitter conflict.

The Percies' extensive estates in Northumberland, Yorkshire and Cumberland made them the most powerful family in the north. By the 1530s the sixth earl had built up what seemed an impregnably dominating hold on the area, through his wardenship of the east and middle marches and his lieutenancy in Yorkshire. He was also sheriff of Northumberland for life. But his position in relation to the crown was in fact perilous. He was estranged from his wife and had no heir. He was regarded with the deepest suspicion in London because of his prestige in the north. A precontract of marriage with Anne Boleyn made him insecure when the divorce became an issue. He was on bad terms with his brother, Sir Thomas, whom Henry in any case objected to as his heir in 1535. This is the background to Northumberland's eccentric and sensational gesture of 1536: he made the king his sole heir. This was his means of escape from the appalling dilemma of the great magnate faced with a suspicious master. In 1535 he made approaches to Chapuys; throughout the previous decade he had tried to fortify his position in the north by the multiplication of offices and fees. Now he took provision for an alternative to the extreme risks inherent in rebellion (**99**, pp. 171–2).

After this it was impossible for Northumberland to emerge as a leader of the pilgrims. Publicly he remained aloof throughout the rising; in fact he quietly forwarded it, surrendering Wressle castle to Aske and recognising him as 'captain of the baronage'. While the earl was still in London in early October the commons had shouted 'thousands for a Percy' at the castle gate; elsewhere in the north his family quickly became the obvious leaders. Sir Ingram, constable of Alnwick Castle, led the company from Northumberland. Sir Thomas, who marched to York with the commons of the East Riding, was referred to as 'the lock, key and wards of this matter'. He blamed Cromwell for depriving him of his inheritance. When he entered York the commons 'showed such affection towards him as they showed towards none other. Gorgeously he rode through the city in complete harness with feathers trimmed as well as he might deck himself at that time'. When the allegiances of the captains of the pilgrimage are examined an impressively large number of them turn out to be Percy tenants. Four were actually members of Northumberland's council: Aske was his legal adviser, Sir Robert Constable was lord of Flamborough and thirty-six other manors, and Robert Lascelles and William Stapleton were holders of important Percy estates (**96**, pp. 7–9).

If the Pilgrimage was to a large extent a Percy rising, in Craven, Cumberland and Westmorland it was also a rising by the commons against the hated Earl of Cumberland. The crisis of 1536 saw his authority in the north dramatically collapse. By then he had alienated his mesne tenants, those gentry who held of him as freeholders by knight service, by his efforts to exploit them financially and his failure to give a firm lead as Warden of the West Marsh. He had also alienated his customary tenants by his exacting agrarian policies. As a result he found himself besieged in Skipton castle and deserted by his gentry retinue. His attackers included gentry from the North Riding such as Richard Norton. Among the commons 'no man was worse beloved' than Cumberland.

To the Percies the crisis of 1536 was an ideal opportunity to harness the resentment of the Commons in their quarrel with the rival Cliffords. The evidence that they did this, if not conclusive, is at least very suggestive. In 1535, when many Percy tenants took part in the riots in Craven, Northumberland was reluctant to suppress the disorder. He may have even encouraged the tenants of Winterburn, whom Cumberland had illtreated, to resist the earl's oppressions. The next year the rising in Craven began on Percy estates at Giggleswick. And Sir Stephen Hammerton, whom the tenants chose as their leader was one of Northumberland's officers. There are hints that the Earl may have been sending him orders as to how to proceed from Wressle (**66; 99,** pp. 162–3, 175, 199–202).

Yet to see the rising too much in terms of the Percy-Clifford feud would be to over-simplify it. R. B. Smith concluded from his analysis of landed income and social structure in the West Riding in this period that the nobility were the most ruthless group of landlords (**79; 99,** pp. 79–80). There is evidence that both Northumberland and Cumberland levied heavy fines and made changes in tenure and customs as a means to improving the profitability of their estates in the years before the Pilgrimage. An examination of the estates of the Percy family has shown that, while entry fines were put on a regular footing at the end of the fifteenth century, they were at first kept at a reasonable level of one or one and a half years' rent (**3**). But some fines were raised in the period 1500–36. The Earl of Cumberland's racking rent was blatant. He had been taking fines of seven to eight years' rent from tenants entering on intakes in his forests of Stainmore and Mallerstang. It was no coincidence that the rising flared up at Kirkby Stephen, in the middle of the Clifford lands and these forests. Neither of the earls can be exonerated from the charge that they failed to observe the good lordship which was essential to the harmony of a society which still had strong feudal elements. The Duke of Norfolk recognised this when he reported to Cromwell in 1537 that Cumberland 'must be brought to change his conditions and not be so greedy to get money of his tenants' before there could be peace in the north-west.

R. B. Smith found that in the most restive areas in 1536 and the areas where the initial disturbances took place the nobility and the church held more than their average share of land. He also found that the evidence of taxation records showed these areas to be among the poorest in the West Riding. Marshland and the south-east parts of the Riding had declined considerably in wealth since the fourteenth century. Dentdale and Sedbergh had already resisted royal taxation in 1513. The general poverty of the western dales is not in doubt. In 1537 Norfolk reported the desperate poverty of the Lake Counties: 'What the gressing of them so marvellously sore in time past and with increasing of lords rents by inclosings . . . this border is sore weked and specially Westmoreland.' Article 9 in the Pontefract manifesto must be seen against this background. The demand for tenant right, the succession of their family to their lands without unreasonable exactions, reflects the extreme insecurity of the commons position in the face of grasping landlords.

The enclosure article likewise must be seen in the context of the tradition of landlord-tenant conflict on enclosure in the north in the early sixteenth century (article 13). This article together with the one on entry fines was extracted by Aske from the petition of the Westmorland commons because, although these grievances were concentrated west of the Pennines, they were of concern to all areas of the north. Sixteen cases of popular rioting and unrest over enclosure in the north reached the courts in the period 1528–47. The York commons were involved in enclosure riots in 1534, 1536 and 1546 but enclosure seems to have been a serious grievance mainly in the uplands, where loss of common land deprived men of their pasture rights (**41,** p. 220; **96,** p. 9). Cornland was scarce in the congested valleys of north-west Yorkshire, Cumberland and Westmorland and tenants relied for their livelihood on their grazing rights on the fells (**64**). There was, it seems, severe pressure of population on land in this area. This is suggested by the extensive settlement of forests in the early sixteenth century. By 1537 only sixty deer survived in Ribblesdale and 'little timber or other wood'.

When land was scarce and gentry exploited it in their own interest social resentment quickly came to the surface. There was talk in Cumberland and Westmorland of killing the gentry and there were a few attacks on their property. Sir James Laborne of Kendal had his house spoiled because of his reputation for sharply increasing entry fines. On the other hand two prominent Cumberland gentry attended the commons musters. It would be wrong to see the rising as in any real sense a peasant war.

The Westmorland commons' letter to Lord Darcy mentioned a number of grievances that did not appear in the final manifesto, presumably because Aske did not consider them sufficiently important [**doc. 7**]. As a result some interesting light on the discontents of the commons west of the Pennines has been little noticed by historians of the Pilgrimage. The traditional feudal dues of 'neat geld' and 'serjeant corn', could undoubtedly be a serious burden to customary tenants who were already obliged to give border service against the Scots. The Westmorland commons also seemed to envisage the abolition of tithes. This demand reflects the strong vein of anticlericalism running through their letter to Lord Darcy. The commons expressed dissatisfaction with many of their priests; in a remarkable outburst of radical thinking they went so far as to suggest that they themselves might take the initiative in replacing inadequate or non-resident ministers. Here is an early hint of the seeds from which congregationalism might grow. It was echoed more stridently in 1549 in a rebellion that was openly protestant in tone. It confirms the extreme complexity of the movement Aske managed to hold together (**99,** pp. 204–5).

Until more research has been done on the local sources of the Pilgrimage, any analysis of it must leave a number of questions unanswered. The role of the prophecies and ballads, which circulated in the north and acclimatised the commons to the possibilities of drastic action, deserves closer investigation (**10, 11, 12**). The Pilgrimage of Grace was the popular response of a large body of Englishmen to the dramatic and innovating policies of the Henrician Reformation (**97,** pp. 339–41). As such it illuminates more vividly than any other Tudor rebellion the attitudes of ordinary men and women to an explosive period of Tudor government.

HENRY VIII AND THE NORTH, 1537–47

After the negotiations at Doncaster the king's policy was to divide the gentry from the commons, and harry the north with propaganda on the sinfulness of rebellion. He was waiting his chance for revenge. This was provided by the rising led by the protestant Sir Francis Bigod, in the East Riding on 16 January. Aske at this time was telling the northern gentry of the promises he had been given in London of a parliament in the north and a visit by the king. Bigod alone perceived the hollowness of the government's pardon. Because he did not believe it was valid he evolved, with the pilgrim captain John Hallam, a plan to capture Hull and Scarborough. If Norfolk came north he could be taken and used as an intermediary with the government. Professor Dickens regards Bigod's scheme as 'the most interesting politico-military concept evolved by a Tudor rebel' (**10**).

The outcome was pathetic and disastrous. Bigod had failed to make the minimum of contacts necessary among the local gentry. The few hundred commons who mustered briefly, held Beverley, after failing to capture Hull or Scarborough. Within a few days Bigod was a hunted fugitive. He was captured in Cumberland on 10 February. Here in February the commons mustered on their own initiative because their patience with the gentry had run out. They were routed in an attack on Carlisle.

These two outbursts of disorder gave Henry the excuse he needed to pursue a systematic policy of punishment. The Duke of Norfolk declared martial law in the West March, and rebels were hanged at Carlisle and in the Cumberland villages. During the spring, the gentry leaders were gradually rounded up, brought to London and tried. A total of 178 executions are recorded (**85,** pp. 387–9). Among the gentry who were executed were Sir Thomas Percy, Sir Stephen Hammerton and Sir Francis Bigod. Lord Darcy was beheaded on 30 June. And on 12 July Robert Aske was drawn to his execution on Clifford's Tower at York. On the scaffold he made a confession characteristic of Henrician subjects about to die for treason: 'The King's Majesty, he said, he had greatly offended in breaking his laws whereunto every true subject is bounden by the commandment of God.'

In May 1537 Northumberland, unhappy under the shadow of treason, made over all his lands unconditionally to the crown. With his death in July, Henry had achieved the object for which he had been striving: the destruction of the Percy interest. But it was clear from the Duke of Norfolk's harping on the need to have 'men of estimation and nobility' to rule the Marches that he too had ambitions to be an overmighty subject. Rather than take any such risk Henry now accelerated his policy of building up a royal interest in the north, by giving increased authority to gentry families who had served him loyally. 'If it shall please his majesty', wrote the Council to Norfolk, 'to appoynt the meanest man to rule and govern in that place, is not his Graces authoritie sufficient to cause al men to serve his Grace under him without respect of the verie estate of the personage.' Henry added a note to this himself: 'For surely we woll not be bound of a necessitie to be served with lordes. But we woll be served with such men what degree soever as we shall appoint to the same.' In the appointment of Sir Thomas Wharton to the Wardenry of the West March in 1544 we can see Richard Morrison's arguments for the claims of virtue above rank being put into practice [**doc. 10**]. Wharton's qualification was that the king trusted him and he was an able administrator. He obtained the substance of the Warden's power in 1537, thus ending the rule of the Earl of Cumberland in the West March (**64**).

In 1537 also the Council of the North was reorganised and put on a permanent footing (**32, 52, 57**). Many of the pilgrim leaders, men like Sir Thomas Tempest, Sir Ralph Ellerker and Robert Bowes, were among its first members. Thus, through the new council and the rule of men like Sir Thomas Wharton, the Henrician government tried to counteract the endemic violence and lawlessness of the north. Bowes and Ellerker, in a survey of the borders made in 1542, wrote that the borderers 'most prayses and cheryshes suche as begynne sonest in youthe to practise themselves in theftes and robberies contrary to the kinges graces lawes'. In the first decade of its existence the new council not only had to cope with the persistent border feuds, but with the widespread discontent and antagonism to the regime which simmered in the years following the Pilgrimage (**54**). The north's faith in the Percies did not die. While the substance of their power had passed to the king, numerous prophecies circulated foretelling the reawakening of their prestige: 'The moon shall kindle again, and take light of the sun, meaning by the moon the blood of the Percies.' The belief in their return to power was seen in almost magical terms. If anything happened to the king, a Yorkshire tiler told some friends in Kent in 1538, a Percy would inherit and 'he would cause Ingland to shyne as bryght as seynt George' (**85,** pp. 61–4; **100,** pp. 400–1).

Throughout 1537 popular sedition was always near the surface. In March Dr Dakyn, the vicar general of the diocese of York, told the Privy Council that since the rising he had exhorted the people of Richmond to accept the royal supremacy only at the risk of his life. The Duke of Norfolk found it necessary to attend the suppression of Bridlington and Jervaulx in person because the neighbouring country was populous and the houses were 'greatly beloved'. Then in 1541 a new plot emerged, led by a small group of gentry and the clergy of the Wakefield district. The plan was to kill Robert Holgate, the President of the Council of the North and hold Pontefract castle till help came from Scotland. The plot was caused by resentment at the punishments following the 1536 rising and the government's continuance of policies which were obnoxious to the north. The drive against the great abbeys and the seigneurial franchises in the years 1537–41 meant that by 1541 Aske's fears that the north would be drained of currency were being at least partially realised [**doc. 5**]. In 1540 the crown drew £6,110 from land in the West Riding which had belonged a short time before to the church or other laymen (**79**). Fifty to a hundred people seem to have been involved in the plot, of whom about fifteen were executed. There is little evidence that it engaged popular feeling on any scale (**99,** p. 210).

The swift discovery and crushing of the Wakefield plot demonstrated the utility of the new Council of the North. Yet, coinciding with new Scottish border raids, it caused Henry serious concern. He started to adopt a more friendly attitude to France. He took measures to strengthen the border towns against the Scots. Then in the summer he made a lavish progress to the north, hoping to overawe it with his royal person (**96,** p. 12; **97,** pp. 427–8). This seems to have worked. For the last six years of his reign there were no further plots and no cases of treason. Temporarily at least the north was tamed. But the absence of internal unrest in this period is only one side of the picture. The experiment of relying upon old border gentry, such as Sir Thomas Wharton and William Eure, as wardens was a failure. Since both had difficulties in securing military co-operation from the English borderers, the Henrician government was driven to rely increasingly during the 1540s on paid garrisons and foreign mercenaries to defend its northern frontier. The far north remained a pressing military and administrative problem (**82**).

5 The Western Rebellion

RIOT AND REBELLION IN THE WEST 1547–9

The first insurrections of the Cornishmen against the Edwardian Reformation, in 1547 and 1548, sprang from fear of the loss of church goods and the intense unpopularity of the government's agent, William Body. Body was an unscrupulous and avaricious careerist. He had obtained the archdeaconry of Cornwall in 1537 from Thomas Wynter, Wolsey's illegitimate son, who was in debt to him. The Bishop of Exeter challenged Wynter's right to transfer the archdeaconry to Body for a term of thirty-five years, and in 1541 the bishop's agents tried to prevent his collection of the clergy's procurations at Launceston. Body replied by a writ of praemunire against the bishop's official which was successful.

When Body returned to the county in 1547 and summoned the clergy to hear the Edwardian injunctions he met with a hostile demonstration at Penryn which thoroughly alarmed the authorities. The college of St Mary and St Thomas at Glasney just outside Penryn was the largest religious foundation remaining in the county at this time with a revenue of £221 a year. It seems Body gave the impression that the inventories which the commissioners who were surveying the chantries were taking of church goods, implied that they would be confiscated. The government dealt mildly with the disturbance on this occasion, and showed themselves anxious to appease the commons.

The next year Body was back in Cornwall visiting the parish churches to ensure that the government's orders on the destruction of all images were being carried out. When Body arrived at Helston on 6 April, a mob, led by Martin Geoffrey, the priest of the rebellious parish of St Keverne, set upon him and killed him. The Cornishmen had demonstrated their readiness to take the law into their own hands against an official they disliked and with whom they identified the new religious policy. The murder of Body was the first violent expression of their hostility to the demolition of traditional rituals which the move towards Protestantism involved. John Resseigh, the yeoman leader of the mob, took his stand on the 'laws and ordinances touching the Christian religion' as they existed at the death of Henry VIII 'of blessed memory'. He challenged the right of a protector to alter these laws. This could only be done by the king when he had come of age which, so far as Resseigh was concerned, was when he was twenty-four. That was thirteen years away. Meanwhile, Resseigh proclaimed defiantly in Helston market place, 'whosoever dare defend this Body and follow such new fashions as he did, we will punish him likewise'.

Such was the temper of the commons that the Justices cancelled the sessions to be held at Helston and arranged for those of the ringleaders who they had managed to arrest to be tried at Launceston. The gentry had no hold over the far west and called on Sir Richard Edgecombe, one of the principal Devon gentry, to come to their aid. He collected men from the parishes in the east of the county on his way. But the victimisation of Body had, for the moment, satisfied the commons. The trouble died down and men returned to their homes. The government issued a general pardon excepting twenty-eight of the ringleaders. Only ten of these were in fact hanged (**91,** pp. 439–40).

During the next year the religious policies initiated by Protector Somerset continued to make their impact on the county. The government made some attempt to be constructive: when the chantries were dissolved arrangements were made for the continuance of four schools and for curacies in the larger parishes. A preacher was sent to begin the conversion of the county. But the atmosphere remained unsettled and even the boys of Bodmin school divided themselves into two factions, those who supported the old religion and those who supported the new. Their escapades led to them blowing up a calf and them all being beaten.

It was the rumours of the simplification of the liturgy in the new prayer book to be enforced on Whitsunday 1549 that turned the Cornish opposition into a full-scale rebellion. The commons from the villages around Bodmin persuaded Humphrey Arundell, a man with extensive estates in that area, to be their leader. He was clearly a troublemaker since he had appeared in a number of Chancery cases charged, among other things, with forcible entry upon other people's lands. The only other gentleman involved was John

Winslade of Tregarrick. The rebels collected at Bodmin where they formed a camp. The articles drawn up there were very likely the work of the small group of priests, whose influence held the rebels together and with Arundell's organisation gave the rising a defined purpose. Early in June the rebels advanced into Devon leaving a small force to besiege Plymouth.

In Devon the rising began independently and spontaneously at Sampford Courtenay. Here the priest, following the orders of the government, said the new service on Whitsunday, 10 June. But the next day the villagers persuaded him to defy the government. John Hooker, who wrote the only detailed contemporary account of the rebellion, recounts that he 'yielded to their wills and forthwith raversheth himself in his old popish attire and sayeth mass and all such services as in times past accustomed'. The Devonshire Justices of the Peace lacked the confidence and authority to impose the government's will; they could do nothing to prevent such outrages as the murder of one of the gentry who urged the people to remain peaceful and obedient. The Sampford Courtenay men and others from villages around joined the Cornishmen at Crediton, where by 20 June a considerable force had gathered.

When news of the rebellion reached the court the government hastily summoned Sir Peter Carew from Lincolnshire, where he was living on his wife's estates. He had served Henry VIII at court and in France, had sat as M.P. for Tavistock in 1545 and been sheriff of Devon in 1547. He was chosen as the man believed to have most influence in the county and best fitted to deal energetically but leniently with the rebels. By 21 June he had reached Exeter. When he had discussed the situation with the sheriff and J.P.s he rode to Crediton with a small company to try to pacify the rebels. He found the town defended and they refused to negotiate. However, one of Carew's men set fire to the farms which formed part of the rebel defences. Wild panic ensued, and the town was abandoned. This incident merely increased the distrust between gentry and commons: 'the noise of this fire and burning', relates Hooker, 'was spread through the villages and the common people noised and spread it abroad that the gentlemen were altogether bent to over-run, spoil and destroy them'.

The main army of the rebels moved round Exeter to Clyst St Mary, where by 23 June they had made camp and fortified the bridge on the Exeter road. The gentry then made another attempt

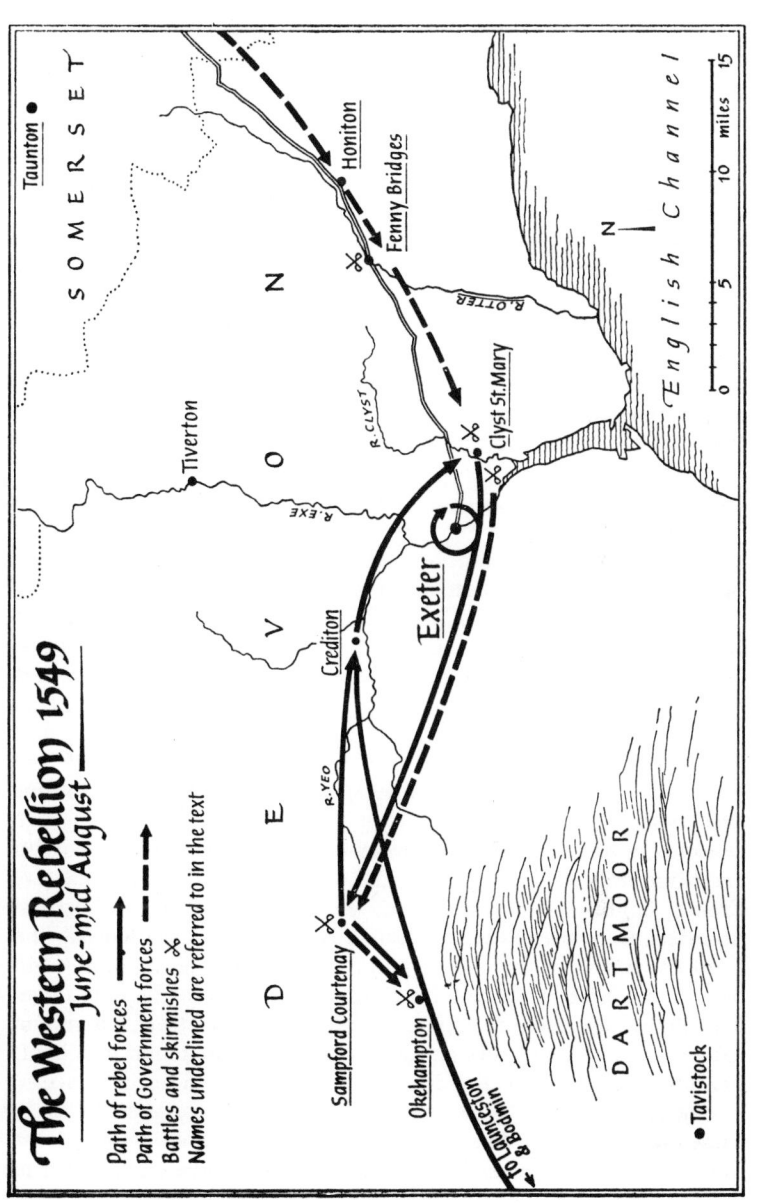

The Western Rebellion 1549
June–mid August

Path of rebel forces
Path of Government forces
Battles and skirmishes ✕
Names underlined are referred to in the text

to open negotiations. This time two of them, Sir Thomas Denys and Sir Hugh Pollard, were allowed into the village. They showed some sympathy with the rebels' demand that religion should remain as Henry VIII left it until Edward came of age. They extracted a promise from the commons that they would pursue their grievances by petition in an orderly manner. But Sir Peter Carew and Sir Peers Courtenay, the sheriff, were dissatisfied with this, blaming Denys and Pollard 'for theire slender or rather synester dealinges'. That night, the commons, encouraged by this disagreement between the gentry, started to block the highways into Exeter. They were now determined to force Carew to hear their case. They took and imprisoned some of the Exeter merchants and gentry. Others left the city or 'secretelie kepte theireselffes close in certeyne howses then unknowne'. Carew himself escaped and took the road for London to impress on the government the gravity of the situation.

Somerset's policy had, from the beginning, been one of extreme lenience. We do not know how much information he had before him but he certainly did not regard the western disturbance at this stage as a serious rebellion. On 20 June he ordered the sheriff of Devon to pardon all those who had taken part in the Sampford Courtenay commotion but to arrest any who continued to 'repugne or resist our godly procedyngs'. He was anxious to emphasise that his policy had full parliamentary backing and declared his belief that the rebellion arose 'rather of ignorance then of malice, and at the nocion of some light and naughty persons then of any evill will that our loving subjects doth bear to us or to our procedynges'.

Somerset's resources were already strained. He was faced with enclosure riots in the midlands and south-east and feared that the French might take advantage of the opportunity offered by the disorders to invade [**doc. 15**]. On 24 June he sent Lord Russell, the Lord Privy Seal, to the west to ensure its 'good order and quiet', but he was only able to provide him with a small and inadequate force. Russell was ordered to pay particular attention to the arrest of rumour-mongers and the setting up of beacons. He found it difficult to enlist forces in Wiltshire and Somerset and dared not advance to Exeter. On 29 June the earl of Arundell wrote to Sir William Petre from Guildford that 'these parts remayn as well as may be in a quaveryng quyet'. It seems that at this time a force determined to march on London would have had little difficulty in passing to the north of Russell by Bruton or to the south through Dorset. It might have received considerable additional strength as it approached the capital. Russell even talked of retreat: 'if we be driven to retire it standeth uncertayn to us hitherto by what quarter we shall most conveniently use the same until their determinations of proceeding more evidently appear.'

But the rebels were more concerned to demonstrate their seriousness by controlling the west country than to appear in person before London. Perhaps the memory of Blackheath frightened them or perhaps the leaders' nerve failed at the prospect of advancing into unknown country. From Clyst, between 24 June and 2 July, they turned their faces back to Exeter. They sent a further and more detailed set of articles to the Council and coordinated their plans for a full scale seige of the local capital [**doc. 12**]. The leadership now consisted of three Cornish gentry, three Devon gentry and three commoners. On 2 July the rebels, 2,000 in number according to Hooker, advanced in procession on Exeter. They carried the banner of the Five Wounds, the pyx and censers; when the mayor refused their demand for support they surrounded the city.

Somerset's letters show that at this time he was hopelessly out of touch with the situation. He continued to insist on appeasement. He seems even to have considered delaying the enforcement of the new Prayer Book [**doc. 15**]. The siege of Exeter began while the government still hoped to remedy the situation by such stratagems as sending spies among the rebels to emphasise 'the terror of comytting treason, the feare of a kyng's execution'.

It was not until about 10 July that Somerset took the rebellion seriously enough to begin trying to divert some of his forces to help Russell. His answer to their articles, written on behalf of the king on 8 July, was a last attempt to persuade them of the error into which they had been led and to overawe them by the threat of vengeance. Meanwhile Exeter was under siege and because the government's forces were so heavily committed elsewhere it was six weeks before Russell could relieve it. The city was able to defy the rebels during that time because loyalty to the crown overcame religious conviction. There was a tradition of religious conservatism in Exeter. Hooker, who provides an eye-witness account of the siege, explains that the party 'of the old stamp and of the Romish religion' was larger than the protestant group; on the other hand, the magistrates and chieftains of the city albeit they were not fully resolved and satisfied in religion yet they not respecting that but chiefly their dutifulness to the king and commonwealth, nothing liked the rebellion . . . but . . . do all things to defend the city and themselves against their rebellious attempts.

During the siege the citizens maintained contact with Russell through spies, but they were always in danger of being betrayed by one of their own number. A hundred citizens made a covenant to be about the city day and night to prevent any treachery. A plan by the catholic party to allow the rebels in at a postern gate of the castle was only just discovered in time and two days before the city's deliverance the catholics tried to raise a riot in the streets. Hooker emphasises the tension between the two religious groups: when the Mayor held a muster of all the commons in armour at the Guildhall rioting nearly broke out.

There were several violent clashes with the beseigers. When they tried to set fire to the gates the citizens used their ordinance against them charged with 'greate bagges of flynte stones and hayle shote'. A mine laid by the rebels under the city wall had to be flooded by a tinner. By the beginning of August there was danger of famine and the commons were 'verie impaciente to endure the countynnall barkinge of theire hungrie bellies'. Morale was maintained by careful provision for poor relief organised by the mayor and aldermen.

Early in July Russell had advanced to Honiton but, short of money and men, he felt thoroughly insecure; 'having but a very small guard about him', says Hooker, 'he lived in more fear than was feared, for the rebels daily increased and his company decreased and shrank away and he not altogether assured of them which remained'. On 12 July Somerset had to report to Russell that the horsemen and footmen under Lord Grey that he had promised, had been sent instead to deal with a 'sturr here in Bucks and Oxfordshire by instigacon of sundery preists for these matyers of religion'. Somerset was now alarmed; the rebellion in the west took second place to disturbances nearer the capital. But he no longer underestimated the extent of disloyalty in the west and appreciated Russell's anxiety and caution. He advised him not to trust the local gentry 'onles ye knowe them fully perswayded for the matier in contraversie of relygon'; he should 'wink at the matter' of Sir John Arundell who refused to bring forces to Russell's assistance from Dorset.

Russell, left to fend for himself, managed to get the backing of three Exeter merchants to raise money through the merchants of Taunton and Bristol. But his most serious problem remained the unwillingness of the men of Dorset and Somerset to join his army [**doc. 16**]. He maintained in a letter to the Council on 18 July that, with only 1,000 footmen and 700 horses at the maximum, he could neither relieve the city nor resist a rebel advance. He constantly urged Somerset to send more forces. The Protector returned promises of assistance but again was forced to change his plans: the 'mayne force' at one time intended for the west under Lord Warwick, went instead to deal with Kett. By the end of July Somerset's attitude was hardening, or perhaps he was giving way to those on the Council who pressed him to abandon his policy of leniency [**doc. 19**]. A harsher tone entered his letter to Russell on 27 July [**doc. 16**].

Russell began his advance on 28 July. He forced an advance party of rebels to retire from Fenny Bridges after two engagements by the river Otter. The second, says Hooker, was 'sharp and cruel': Russell's men were caught at spoil by a new contingent of Cornishmen and 'many of them paied deerlie for their wares'. The rebels lost about 300 men on this day. Russell continued his advance on 3 August when Lord Grey had arrived with his horsemen and 300 Italian mercenaries. This time the rebels defended Clyst St Mary with about 6,000 men but again they were forced to abandon their position when the mercenaries fired the houses. The next day the final battle was fought on Clyst Heath, the besiegers of Exeter were drawn off and defeated, and those who escaped vanished quickly into the west country lanes.

On 6 August Russell reached the walls of Exeter. The mayor came out to greet him and the King's standard of the red dragon was set up on the city walls. Hooker describes the city's joy; some died, he says, of overeating. Now at last Sir William Herbert arrived with 1,000 men, mainly Welshmen and they helped gather in food and cattle for the city from the surrounding countryside. Russell followed Somerset's orders that he should make an example of the ringleaders, the more important of whom were to be sent to London, but pardon the common people involved in the rebellion. So the vicar of the church of St Thomas was hanged on a gallows erected on his church tower in his vestments, with 'a holy-water bucket, a

55

sprinkle, a sacring bell, a pair of beads and such other like popish trash hanged about him'.

Russell could proclaim the victory of protestantism in Exeter but, despite his now formidable army, he did not feel sufficiently confident to advance into the disordered far west. The breakdown of local government in Devon and Cornwall had now lasted almost two months. Russell wrote to Somerset that to restore control it would be necessary to land 1,000 men at Plymouth 'at the backs of the rebells'. Then, while he delayed in Exeter during the second week of August, beset by problems of money and supplies, he heard that the rebels had re-established their camp at Sampford Courtenay. He was by this time being pressed by Somerset to dismiss at least some of his forces so that the gentry might be at home to defend the south coast counties. With both the West and East Anglia in rebellion, the French declaration of war on 8 August had come at a moment of disturbing internal weakness. In a letter of 14 August Somerset warned that 'yf you shall suffer those rebells to breathe' they might make a further stand or even cooperate with a French invasion.

Somerset was unnecessarily frantic since the rebels lacked the organisation to hold Plymouth, which they had taken earlier in the summer, and were not even in contact with the French. But they showed courage and determination in facing the overwhelming royal army of about 8,000 men that marched west from Exeter on 16 August. The final struggle at Sampford Courtenay was prolonged. Arundell caught the royal troops in the rear and it required a three-fold attack by Russell, Grey and Herbert in the evening to force the rebels to retire. Many were captured and killed in the chase that followed that night and in the engagements when groups of rebels turned to fight in Somerset and at Okehampton; about 4,000 west country men are said to have died at the hands of the royal army.

The rebellion never had a real chance of forcing the government to make concessions in its religious policy. Somerset might have been prepared to do so but under the stress of the sedition of the summer of 1549 he was rapidly losing his grip on the Council. Because the western rising coincided with the Norfolk and Oxfordshire commotions its suppression was prolonged. At another time forces could have reached Exeter much more quickly and the rebellion might not have achieved the proportions or significance it did (**91,** pp. 453–77).

THE REBELLION AND THE EDWARDIAN REFORMATION

The Edwardian Council always regarded the Western Rebellion as primarily religious in purpose. On 11 June Somerset spoke of an attempt, instigated by 'seditious priests, to seke restitucion of the olde bluddy lawes'. The chroniclers' unanimous emphasis on the religious motivation of the rebels is confirmed by their articles, a manifesto for a return to catholicism [**doc. 12**].

That the government took this challenge seriously can be seen from the trouble they went to in answering the rebel demands by three replies. Somerset's reply on behalf of the King dealt with the first set of articles drawn up at Bodmin. These contained the substance of articles 2, 3, 4, 6, 7, 8 of the rebels' manifesto, together with demands that clerical celibacy should be enforced and that the bishop should be ready to confirm children wherever they asked him. Somerset was conciliatory in approach, pointing out for instance that it was an error to regard confirmation as essential to salvation in the same way as baptism. 'We be content', he said, 'to use our princely authority like a father to his children.' The most lengthy remonstration with the rebels came from Nicholas Udall. His detailed point-by-point reply to the commons was aggressively protestant in tone but the political propaganda it employed followed closely the themes of Richard Morrison and earlier publicists. In his most emotive passage Udall rehearsed the familiar argument that rebellion leads to anarchy [**doc. 14**].

Finally there was Archbishop Cranmer's tirade against the rebels, full of his dread of social anarchy and anger at their presumption in addressing their soveriegn so brazenly (**82,** p. 361). While Aske and Kett used the language of petitioners the western commons began each article with the words 'We will have'. 'Was this the manner of speech', Cranmer asked, ' at any time used of the subjects to their Prince since the beginning of the world?' (**33,** p. 293) An anàlysis of these three replies will place the rebellion in the context of the religious changes of 1549.

The government propagandists were throughout at pains to impress upon the commons how they had been deceived by their priests, 'whelps of the Romish litter' as Udall called them. Somerset constantly reiterated his attack on the evil men who 'blow these opinions into your head, to finish their own purposes'. Udall took the line that it was his duty, in his sorrow at the way the commons had been seduced, to give them an answer 'how their consciences may be satisfied and stayed'. He answered their confused and emotional traditionalism with the voice of the convinced protestant who believed in the new order [**doc. 14**]. He based his case, as did Somerset, on 'the sincere word of God set forth by the king's majesty and his most godly council, not only with long study and travail of the best learned bishops and doctors of the realm but also with the assent and consent of the universal clergy and the whole parliament'. So confident was he in his cause that he appealed to the verdict of history.

In answer to the ambiguous reference to 'our forefathers' in the first article Udall put forward the authority of Moses and the prophets; to the general councils of the medieval church he opposed the Councils of the Apostles [**doc. 12**]. He then derided the rebels' rash pronouncements against heresy, which he said they did not understand. Cranmer maintained that the first article was traitorous and contradicted in its support for Rome 'the old ancient laws and customs of this realm'. It was inspired, he said, by the priests' desire for benefit of clergy: 'If a priest had slain one of your sons or brethren, that you should have no remedy against him, but only before the bishop.'

Udall took up the theme of the self-interest of the priesthood in his comments on the Six Articles which the rebels would have had restored (article 2). He attacked the 'mischief wrought' by 'their confession auricular' and 'their sacrament of the altare' and descended quickly to crude anticlerical propaganda: with the end of auricular confession 'is cut from them all opportunity of moving men's wives to folly, of enticing men's daughters to lewdness and vice'. Udall then contrasted the chasteness of clerical marriage, advocated in the scriptures as 'holy and honourable afore God', with the fornication practised by priests. He argued that the Six Articles constituted a temporary measure now abrogated by consent of the whole realm through parliament. Somerset emphasised the king's determination to enforce statute law: 'For herein indeed resteth our honour, herein standeth our kingdom, herein do all kings acknowledge us a king.'

It was not difficult for Udall and Cranmer to ridicule the conservatism expressed by articles 3 and 8. 'Had you rather', asked Cranmer, 'be like pies or parrots, that be taught to speak, and yet understand not one word what they say, than be true christian men that pray unto God in heart and faith?' Surely, they both scornfully asked, there were more Cornishmen who understood English than Latin. If they had made a humble petition to the king to have the new service translated into Cornish, Udall told the rebels, they might have achieved their purpose. 'But', he went on, harking back to their presumption, 'we Cornishmen utterly refuse this new English were too much for a parishioner to say to his curate, or a neighbour to his constable; much more too much it is for subjects so to say to any rulers or governors.' Cranmer tried to show the rebels that the catholic rituals they were used to were much more like the games and pastimes of the Christmas season than the new service which was based on scripture: the priest speaking aloud in Latin, 'and some walking up and down in the church, some saying other prayers in Latin, and none understandeth other'.

The government writers set about condemning the ritualism (article 4) and superstition (article 7) of the rebels by citing biblical passages and decrees of the early church. Honorious III, Cranmer admitted, had decreed that the sacrament should be reserved in order that the priest could take it to the sick but he had not mentioned hanging it over the altar. This, Udall maintained, was merely a convenient solution to the problem of keeping the sacrament when 'by negligence of the curates and parsons, sometimes it moulded and putrified, sometimes it was eaten up with myce or other vermin'. It was never 'decreed by any constitution of the Church'. Yet the western rebels would have had all who would not consent to this practice to 'dye lyke heretykes'. To refute the demand for annual communion by the laity (article 5) Udall quoted extensively from the decrees of general Councils to show that 'Christian men ought to go very often to the most holy communion'. Cranmer, attacked holy water (article 7) as a superstition fabricated by the Papacy. He quoted the second commandment to show that image worship was idolatry.

On the question of the ministration of baptism (article 6) Somerset made it clear to the rebels in his first reply to them that, as 'the first leaf of that part which treateth of baptism' in the new prayer book showed, the government had no intention of confining baptism to Sundays. They had no wish to deprive any dying child of salvation. But, as Cranmer pointed out, there were sound arguments for normally receiving new members into the Church when the whole community was assembled on Sunday; all could rejoice in the new member and all would be reminded of the promises they had made at baptism.

We do not know to what extent Englishmen still believed in purgatory in 1549. It has been suggested that 'a marked decline of interest, a more secular and sceptical attitude, was beginning to manifest itself even before the rise of Protestant beliefs' (**12,** p. 207). But there is evidence that the west was very conservative in this matter: the Cornishmen had expressed their displeasure at the loss of the college at Glasney and, in their demand for the restoration of two abbeys in each county, showed their belief in the efficacy of prayer for 'the King and the Commonwealth' (article 14). The ninth article, on masses for the dead, is the only one that touches on a doctrinal issue. It is interesting that it relates to a belief that impinged closely on the lives of both laity and clergy. For the former the naming of lost friends and relations in church offered comfort and hope; for the latter the dissolutions of 1548 had deprived them of their most valuable vested interest. Udall answered this article by expounding predestination doctrine: 'As for change of God's sentence and judgment there can none be after this life. But (as the scripture saith) where every tree falleth there shall it bee'.

The rebels' objection to the open Bible (article 10), clearly inspired by the priests, provided Udall with another opportunity to display his militant protestanism. He vigorously attacked the catholic priests who had led the people to 'embrace superstition and idolatory for true worship of God, the puddleway and suddes of mennes tradicions for the pure and clere fountain of the Apostles' ordinances'. The rebels' insistence that Dr Moreman should be sent to minister to them (article 11) was probably due to the energy he had shown when, as Vicar of Menheniot in Henry VIII's reign, he had kept a school there. He had been active in teaching the people the Lord's Prayer, the Ten Commandments and the Creed in accordance with Cromwell's injunctions. But Cranmer severely reminded the rebels that it was not the office of a godly prince to give the people teachers who through their catholicism would corrupt them. In the 1530s it had been possible for Cromwell to activate both conservatives and radicals in improving the people's religious knowledge. But by 1549, as the attitudes on both sides of this conflict illustrate, the lines of division had hardened.

SOCIAL AND ECONOMIC CAUSES OF THE REBELLION

The gentleman who wrote to a friend at court from Devon on 27 July 1549 described his difficulties in obtaining an accurate copy of the rebels' articles, 'because they changed them so often, and devysed so many' [**doc. 13**]. He went on to explain the various interests represented in the rebel camp:

The priestes, they harped all upon a playne songe of Rome, certe traytours woulde halow home Cardinall Pole, a nombre of vagabondes wolde have no justice, a bande of theves, wolde have no State of anye Gentlemen and yet to put all in one bagge, a sorte of traytours wolde have nother king nor good subietes. And so every varlet abounded in hys owne sense.

Such an account gives a hopelessly imprecise glimpse of the way the articles were drawn up and the purposes they represented. But it does at least show that to interpret the rebellion as solely religious would be a vast simplification.

The strongest evidence that there was considerable social resentment in the west is article 13 of the demands of the rebels, an attempt to limit the size of gentry households [**doc. 12**]. In a period of dearth and increasing population this did not make sense in economic terms, as Udall pointed out: 'Lette (prevent) gentlemen of their benevolence to keep servants, and where or how shall the rest live?' The article can only be interpreted as an attack on the power and prestige of the western gentry. Cranmer accused the rebels of intending naked class conflict: 'to diminish their strength and to take away their friends, that you might command gentlemen at your pleasures'. A number of incidents during the rebellion confirm the element of class conflict. The murder at Sampford Courtenay was followed by an attempt to capture Sir Walter Raleigh. There was deep distrust of Sir Peter Carew and the Justices throughout the weeks leading up to the seige of Exeter. The commons' promise that they would proceed by petition at Clyst appears to have counted for nothing. This distrust of the gentry is important in explaining the solidarity and determination of the commons throughout June and July. It is evident in the demands for a safe conduct for the captains and for gentry as pledges until the articles were granted in Parliament (articles 15 and 16).

Article 14 is also significant in this context. Cranmer dealt very severely with the suggestion that men should give up any of their abbey or chantry lands (**28,** p. 36). He accused the rebels not only of taking from the King 'such lands as be annexed unto his crown, and be parcel of the same, but also against all right and reason to take from all other men such lands as they came to by most just title, by gift, by sale, by exchange, or otherwise'. The Devon letterwriter was even more incensed at the prospect of giving up his new possessions 'at a papistes appoyntment' [**doc. 13**]. His attitude must have been typical of many gentry who had a vested interest in the progress of the Reformation. 'There is no respect nor difference had amongst you, whether the lands came to them by right or wrong.' Here Cranmer saw the crux of the matter. The gentry identified themselves and the Tudor state with the authority of statute law set forth by the king in parliament. The commons' demands were an open challenge to that authority. And in this article, with its request 'that we may name half of the Commissioners' for the restoration of two abbeys in each county, the challenge was particularly explicit.

More widespread rioting and rebellion occurred in 1549 than any other year in the Tudor century (**41,** p. 223). Much of this sedition, including the rebellion in Norfolk, was economically motivated. Prices had leapt to a new peak (**69**). Protector Somerset continually reiterated in his letters to the west that money was 'never so dear'. By a proclamation of 2 July, which the sheriffs were ordered to proclaim in every market town, Justices were given power to fix prices for victuals and to force farmers and drovers to bring goods to market where there was dearth. This is the background to the western commons' opposition to the tax on sheep and cloth imposed by an act of parliament of March 1549. One set of their articles included a demand that this should be remitted; Somerset was concerned to conciliate the West on this point [**doc. 15**].

The idea of the tax was put forward by John Hales as a revenue device in place of purveyance (**41,** p. 222). He had made careful estimates of the number of sheep in the country and the yield that could be expected from such a tax. He also saw it as a measure to control enclosure, which led to large scale sheep farming. But the incidence of the tax was modified in such a way that it left a heavy burden on the poor, while letting the richer taxpayers off lightly. Hales's intentions were thus frustrated and rumours of the nationwide, parish-by-parish census of sheep that the tax would involve brought bitter resistance in the west and elsewhere. In 1550 the tax was repealed, the preamble explaining that it was too harsh on the poorer commons.

The objection to the census of sheep is the only specifically economic element in the rising. An obscure reference to a tax on geese suggests that rumours of further taxation demands may, as in 1536, have fomented the commons unrest. Yet enclosure, which was the cause of rioting in so many other counties, was almost non-existent in the west (4). Much more detailed local research on the structure and economic relationships of western society is needed before the social basis of the rebellion can be fully explained.

6 Kett's Rebellion

THE REBELLION: JUNE–AUGUST 1549

On 20 June 1549 the villagers of Attleborough in Norfolk threw down the hedges of a local landlord who had enclosed part of their common land. This Attleborough commotion was followed two weeks later by further disturbances, when the whole neighbourhood gathered at the market town of Wymondham for a play to commemorate the translation of Thomas à Becket, to whom the church there was dedicated, to the see of Canterbury. Crowds threw down hedges in nearby villages, including those of Sir John Flowerdew, one of the many successful lawyers among Norfolk gentry. Flowerdew was unpopular in Wymondham because at the dissolution of the abbey there he had stripped the church of its lead roof and carried away the bells. The inhabitants wanted to preserve the church for the town's services. They had in fact bought the choir and monastic buildings.

The manor of Wymondham itself was held of the Earl of Warwick by Robert Kett, whose family had settled there in 1483. He was said to be a tanner by trade but he and his brother William, a butcher, were both landowners of position. Flowerdew hoped to make use of the commons' mood of aggressiveness by persuading them to throw down the hedges of an enclosure of common land Kett had made nearby. His intention was to pursue his feud with the Kett family, who were closely associated with the church he had looted. But the blundering commons found in Robert Kett a leader rather than another victim. Kett agreed that the common land he had enclosed should be made public again and, though his own interest in the enclosure conflict clearly lay with the landlords, said he would stand by the rioters until they had obtained their rights. It was his sense of purpose and capacity for leadership that turned a disorderly riot into a rebellion that was constructive in its ends though disastrous in its outcome.

Kett decided to march to Norwich and he rapidly gained support on the way. He arrived outside the city on 10 July tó find that the news of his coming had led some of the poorer citizens to throw open the hedge round the town close, where the freemen grazed their cattle. By 12 July he had set up camp on Mousehold Heath, a large open hillside just outside the city walls. Within a few days the rebels were said to number 16,000 men.

Little attempt had been made to disperse this massive force of discontented men as Kett led them to Mousehold. At Bowthorpe, Sir Edmund Windham, the High Sheriff of Suffolk and Norfolk, had met them and ordered them in the king's name, to disperse peacefully. He merely irritated them and was lucky to escape unhurt. Sir Roger Wodehouse's intervention was more tactful but no more successful. He met the rebels with three carts laden with beer and provisions which they took from him as well as making him their prisoner.

In Norwich itself there was at first disagreement as to what attitude should be adopted towards a camp of rebellious men who were perhaps greater in numbers than the population within the walls. Those who, like Thomas Codd the mayor, urged moderation, argued that it was unlawful to collect a force without the king's command even to put down rebellion. Anyhow it was impractical; within the city a substantial number of people were sympathetic to Kett.

So, out of fear, Codd and Thomas Aldrich, a man much respected and, says Sotherton, 'of good wisdom and honesty', did their best to cooperate with Kett in his demands for provisions for his men from the city. Sotherton emphasises the restraining influence they were able to have on the hotheads of the camp who looked for further chances to riot. The organisation of the camp and its commissariat depended on the authority of Kett. Codd and Aldrich though also signed both his commission to men to bring in all manner of cattle and provision of victual, and the list of demands which Kett drew up to present to Protector Somerset [**doc. 17**]. On 21 July the government's herald arrived to offer pardon to the rebels if they dispersed. Now the city authorities felt strong enough to act on their own. The mayor and gentry prepared to defend the city and were determined to starve Kett out. Aldermen and their servants kept watch at the gates and six pieces of ordnance were hauled into position on the walls.

The rebels meanwhile had brought in cannon from nearby gentry estates such as Paston Hall. On the night the herald arrived they began their bombardment. This was ineffective because they could do little harm from the top of the hill and when they brought the cannon down nearer the city walls the next morning they feared to use it as they were within range of the city shot. On the third day of open conflict with the city, 23 July, the rebels called for a truce. But when the aldermen refused this they made a full assault armed with spears, swords and pitch forks. Sotherton's account suggests that the ease with which the city was taken in this attack may have been partly due to the reluctance of the gunners to cause wholesale slaughter, which they might have done by using the cannon on the mass of rebels as they swarmed across the river. His attempt to excuse the failure of the archers to repel the rebels is perhaps less convincing and illustrates his characteristic desire to vilify the rebel camp:

> So impudent were they and so desperate that of theyr vagabond boyes (wyth reverens spoken) brychles and bear arssyde came emong the thickett of the arrows and gathered them up when some of the arrows stuck fast in theyr leggs and other parts and did therewith most shamefully turne up their bare tayles agenst those which did shoote, whych soe dysmayed the archers that it tooke theyr hart from them.

By the evening of 23 July Norwich was in the rebels' hands and the herald had left for London. Kett ordered the arrest of the Mayor and Thomas Aldrich who were now kept prisoner at Surrey Place, the mansion on Mousehold Heath of which they had taken possession [**doc. 18**]. But they were allowed some liberty and were treated decently, since Aldwich still had some influence with Kett; the rebel leader knew how much sympathy for Codd and Aldwich there was among the citizens.

On 30 July the Marquis of Northampton arrived outside Norwich with about 14,000 men. He had just been appointed Lord Lieutenant of five eastern counties, including Norfolk. He did not take any immediate initiative towards the rebels but allowed himself to be feasted and entertained by Augustine Steward the Deputy Mayor. The Italian mercenaries Northampton had brought with him 'rested in their armore uppon cushions and pillows'. Meanwhile the rebels managed to capture one of these Italians, 'gorgeously apparelled' says Sotherton, who 'for his apparel sake' was hanged over the walls of Surrey Place. After some cannonading during the night Northampton's trumpeter declared a pardon from the walls to any who would give themselves up. About twenty men came down the hill. The rebels then made a determined attack and a bloody battle followed on the edge of the city. The parish register records the burial of thirty-six men who died; among them was Lord Sheffield, killed by Fulke the butcher.

Panic followed among the gentry when Northampton abandoned his task and left the city: 'Some fled in their doublets and hosen and some in there lightest garments beste to escape and make haste away', relates Sotherton. Once more the rebels were in control of the city and during the next three weeks Kett maintained his camp at Mousehold with the enforced cooperation of the Norwich trades-men. He was at this time sufficiently confident to try to extend his support by winning over Yarmouth. First he sent a small force to persuade them to join him. When they refused, he attacked the town, but he achieved little apart from the destruction of some harbour work in progress; six guns were lost and thirty men taken prisoner.

Meanwhile the government had issued commissions to all shires around Norfolk for levying troops against the rebels; the Earl of Warwick was put in command of the new force, said to be of 12,000 men, which arrived outside Norwich on 23 August. A band of rebels met Warwick's herald and rode with him through the city to Mousehold where the camp was ready in good order to hear his speech. 'They put of theyr caps and cryed God Save King Edward', says Sotherton. The herald offered pardon to all except Robert Kett himself. Despite this the rebel leader was prepared to go with the herald to meet the Earl of Warwick. But some of his followers pulled him back saying, according to Holinshed, 'that he was not the king's herald but someone made out by the gentlemen in such a gaie coate, patched together of vestments and church stuffe, being sent only to deceive them, in offering them pardon'. Distrust of the herald turned to anger and tumult when the cry went up that a boy had been killed by one of the soldiers. The moment when peace had seemed possible had passed.

The next day Warwick and his army entered Norwich and hanged some of the rebels whom they found in the city. The rebels made a desperate attempt to capture some of Warwick's ordnance, attacking the carts with staves and pitchforks. Their tactics against the army in Norwich were arson at night and back street skirmishing in the day time, but as soon as Warwick's arquebusiers were posted throughout the city their training and skill began to tell. One hundred rebels were slain on 24 August. On the fourth day 1,000 foreign mercenaries arrived and Warwick had by then cut some of the camp's supply lines. Kett then became desperate and 'trusted uppon faynid prophecies which were phantastically devised':

> The countrie gruffes, Hob, Dick and Hick
> with clubs and clowted shoone,
> Shall fill up Dufsindale with blood
> of slaughtered bodies soon.

This was the prophesy, Holinshed reports, which Kett followed on the evening of 26 August although it foretold the disaster which was to overwhelm the rebels at Dussindale the next day. The huts and tents at Mousehold were fired and the ordnance was moved to the nearby plain, where trenches were dug and a defensive position was prepared.

Warwick was thus presented with a magnificent chance to use his cavalry. When the rebels had defied Sir Edmond Knyvet, who went forward to ask them to yield, his opening shots killed the horse of the rebel standard-bearer. The undisciplined ranks were quickly mown down and perhaps as many as 3,000 of Kett's men were killed.

Kett himself escaped but was soon caught. He was condemned for treason on 26 November and hanged at Norwich Castle on 7 December. His brother William was hanged from Wymondham steeple. Although Neville states that 300 in all were executed there is clear evidence of only forty-nine paying the penalty for rebellion. For Kett the turning point had been the arrival of the herald on 21 July, with his summons to the camp to disperse. Up till then he believed in the government's support. In the disillusion that followed he could not prevent the unprovoked attack on the city. The extinction of the rebellion became only a matter of time (**91,** pp. 477–93).

THE CAUSES OF THE REBELLION

In a proclamation of 14 June 1549, Edward VI pardoned the 'great number of rude and ignorant people' who had 'riotously assembled themselves, plucked down men's hedges' and 'disparked their parks'. These disorders arose from the unrealistic social policy of Protector Somerset, which was by this time coming under severe criticism [**doc. 19**]. His genuine concern to protect the commons from exploitation is proved by the private Act of parliament he promoted to give security to copyholders on his own estates. He also established a court of requests in his own house to give justice to the poor. But his patronage of John Hales, who introduced three Bills on enclosure into parliament in 1548, quickly aroused the fierce opposition of the landlords and Somerset was forced to resort to administrative action. By 1549 rumours of the proceedings in the midlands of Hales's enclosure commission were spreading to neighbouring counties and the men of Attleborough, living on the main route from Cambridge to Norwich, had plenty of opportunity to hear them. The idea that the government supported the commons in redressing their own grievances, that the 'Good Duke' was on their side, encouraged them to riot.

The returns to Wolsey's commission in 1517 show that a considerable amount of enclosure had taken place in Norfolk in the early years of the century, though in most cases the area enclosed was small, usually under forty acres. Professor Beresford puts forward three 'clear cases' of Tudor depopulation and provisionally assigns twelve other depopulated villages to the Yorkist and Tudor periods (**4,** p. 365). The judicial records provide little evidence of eviction in Norfolk in the period 1500–50 but it is clear that gradual encroachment on the common rights of the peasantry was a serious grievance in a number of villages. By the 1540s the Norfolk peasantry had learned to use the courts of Star Chamber and Requests to defend themselves against encroaching gentry. But there came a point when distrust of the processes of conciliar justice led them to take the law into their own hands.

The inhabitants of Hingham had taken their landlord, Sir Henry Parker, to Star Chamber for infringement of their rights of common pasture on an area of waste land in the village. Failing to receive satisfaction they threatened him with violence and said they would kill the 600 sheep with which he had overstocked the commons. Parker brought an indictment for riot against the tenants in the Norfolk quarter sessions, where they maintained that as freeholders they had common rights as well for 'sheep as for greate beasts'. A similar long drawn out struggle at Great Dunham led to a mob assembling with pitchforks in 1544.

Descriptive Analysis

Throwing down hedges was in fact the easiest and most obvious gesture open to men bewildered by the economic pressures of the time and resentful of the prosperity of their landlords. Kett's rebellion began as an enclosure riot. Because it found a determined leader it became a six week demonstration in defiance of the county. It may be misleading that enclosure is only mentioned once in the articles of the rebels [**doc. 17,** article 1]. Kett was well aware that Somerset was proceeding against enclosers; and as enclosure was often the final stage in the process of invasion of common rights, he must have been in sympathy with the government's aims. Although the article itself is ambiguous, it is best interpreted as showing general approval of the policy the government was assumed to be intending to implement; the request that enclosures that had been made for growing saffron should be retained was an effort to protect a local industry, important to worsted manufacture.

In order to understand the great emphasis given by the rebels to enhancement of rents it is necessary to consider the evidence of inflation provided by Professor Phelps Brown's price index for the Tudor period (**69**). The index measures the comparative cost year by year of a basketful of consumables such as an ordinary family might use. The years 1451–75, a period of stability in prices, are taken as a base period, with the index for these years as 100. There was rapid inflation during Henry VIII's reign caused at least partially by his currency debasements and continental expeditions; by 1548 the index had climbed to 193 and during the years 1548 and 1549 it rose sharply again to 262 in 1550. As prices went up so did rents. The Norfolk rebels had some reason to look back to the 1480s as a golden age before inflation and rackrenting began [**doc. 17,** articles 5, 6, 14 and 17]. In the 1540s landlords tried to pass on as many of their financial obligations as possible. Among these were payments to the crown or superior landlords for lands held of them, referred to in article 2, and such traditional dues, taking their origin in medieval obligations of military service, as 'castillward rent' (article 9).

Rackrenting was certainly felt to be a major and long-standing grievance in Norfolk but there is insufficient evidence to be sure whether rents were ahead of, or merely keeping up with, prices. The figures for the Herbert estates in Wiltshire show that rents per acre on new takings increased more than fivefold in the sixteenth century and it has been suggested that the Herbert rent index 'may be taken as generally applicable to lowland England' (**62**). If this is so, it would appear that Norfolk landlords had no difficulty in keeping pace with such increased expenses as they had to meet; and where landlords were harsh the peasantry undoubtedly suffered hardship.

As we would expect, common rights gain considerable attention in the rebel manifesto (articles 3 and 11). Although the Norfolk peasantry were primarily arable farmers, the light soils of the county made fertiliser indispensable and so rights of pasturing sheep and cattle were essential to their livelihood. But the gentry found the tenurial customs of the county offered them a particularly attractive opportunity to establish large sheep flocks, for which permanent pastures could be obtained by the process of invasion of peasant rights and holdings. This was possible through the foldcourse system which was peculiar to Norfolk. It had developed from the medieval right of foldage, by which landlords could demand that tenants should manure their demesne land by folding flocks of sheep on it at night. Through the foldcourse, the obverse of this, they had a right to pasture their own flocks on their tenant's lands and on common land. In this case the rebels could not back their case by an appeal to 'custom' or 'right'. Kett's request in his final article that the wealthier gentry should not be allowed to 'graze nor fede eny bullocks or shepe . . . but only for the provicion of his howse' is indicative of his determination to challenge the whole practice of large scale sheepfarming in the county, as well as the tenurial system which made it possible. He has been credited with 'a radical programme which would have clipped the wings of rural capitalism' (**50**).

Thomas Townshend was typical of the men earning substantial fortunes at the expense of peasant rights. He built up a flock of 4,000 sheep in the 1540s and his accounts show that his total profits steadily increased from £99 in 1545 to £133 in 1548 (**75; 98**). The lack of entries in the accounts for joysment, the right of pasturing beasts on another's land, suggests that Townshend's method was to use the foldcourse system as a first step towards purchase or eviction. In this way he obtained lands for his own permanent pasture. The large proportion of freeholders and copyholders by inheritance on many Norfolk manors sometimes made eviction difficult. Article 21, on the conversion of freehold land to copyhold, clearly refers to one method of circumventing this hazard in establishing a sheep run.

71

Two articles were particularly aimed at the lawyers of the county, men such as Flowerdew, Hobart of Morley, whose fences were levelled, and John Corbet, who had bought Sprowston chantry in 1548 and had his home and dovecote pillaged by the rebels. Holders of the offices of feodary and escheator were inevitably involved in the very active land market of Edward VI's reign. They thus had exceptional opportunities for self aggrandisement and speculation on behalf of interested parties. When the feodary, the county representative of the Court of Wards reponsible for all matters relating to land held of the king by knight service, was also adviser to a local landlord the results could be thoroughly detrimental to the freedom of the market (article 12). The intention behind article 18 was to save poorer tenants from the expenses involved in an inquisition into their property such as the escheator or feodary might demand. In the light of the fact that the escheator for the county for the past year had been John Flowerdew of Hethersett, the mention of this officer both here and in article 27 may reflect the intrusion into the rebel manifesto of the personal feud of the Ketts and the Flowerdews.

There is no question of the protestant tone of the camp at Mousehold. Thomas Coniers, a Norwich incumbent, daily used the new prayer book, which had only been officially in use a few weeks, at the services held at the Oak of Reformation: Matthew Parker, the future Archbishop, preached there. Norfolk had a strong and longstanding heretical tradition: the Lollards there in Henry VI's reign had tended towards the more radical forms of belief and there were several heresy cases in the early sixteenth century, leading to three burnings in the years 1507–11 (**43**). The persistence of the tradition can be illustrated by some of the cases in the later years of Henry VIII's reign. These confirm that East Anglian popular heresy in the 1540s was, as in the Province of York, still Lollard in atmosphere, rather than Lutheran or Zwinglian (**10**). John Church, a haberdasher of Great Yarmouth who was a sacramentarian, maintained 'that where we have been taught that the sacrement of the altar is flesh and blood we have been taught wrong'. Thomas Baker of Sprowston refused auricular confession saying 'that if he had stollen a horse or a cowe to whom should he go for to be confessed he had no goode go to block nor tree nor to a knave prest to shew hym his confession'. In such cases scepticism of certain Catholic doctrines and anticlericalism were the mainsprings of dissent.

The seven articles in Kett's manifesto which may be classified as religious show that he was constructive in his attitude to the clergy and in his serious concern for their competence. His thinking, in fact, on the role of the clergy in society followed the mainstream of the English Reformation. The complaint in article 15 that priests preferred the comfort of residing in aristocratic households to the simple living of the average benefice, and the dislike of their grasping attitude to tithes expressed in article 22, echo the grievances of the parliament of 1529. The insistence that richer clerics had a duty to 'tech pore men's chyldren of ther paryshe the boke called the cathakysme and the prymer' (article 20) was in line with the Cromwellian injunctions of 1536. The idea that preaching was the essential qualification for the ministry (article 8) reiterated Cromwell's emphasis on the need for quarterly sermons in his injunctions of 1538. More important it looked forward to the popular protestantism of Elizabeth's reign when the 'godly' showed themselves critical of the quality of their clergy and willing to take the initiative in seeking out ministers who were educated and regular preachers. The case in the Mayor's Court at Norwich in 1548 in which a butcher, Thomas Toly, was accused of spreading the idea that the city had a popish priest and wanted to 'pul him out of his foles cote', probably reflects no more than anticlericalism. But in this article Kett made a much more revolutionary suggestion. When a non-preaching minister was replaced 'the parisheners there' might choose another. In this idea we may distinguish an early indication that 'the character of popular protestantism inevitably tended towards congregational independency' (**53, 7,** p. 229).

Clerical involvement in the active Norfolk land market (article 4) may have been a particularly sore local grievance at a time when beneficed clergy who could afford it were offered tempting chances of increased wealth and therefore comfort. Robert Ullathorne of Stockton, for instance was continually acquiring land in his village between 1543–55 and died in possession of the greater part of the manor of Geldeston (**75**). Kett was also aware of the continuing and growing problem of the exploitation of the economic foundations of the church by the gentry (article 26 and 15).

The most remarkable of all the articles is 16: the request that 'all bondemen may be made ffre for god made all ffre with his precious blode sheddying'. Here alone the appeal is based on Christ. It appears also in the Twelve Articles of the German peasant rising of

1525 where serfdom was a real issue. As the demand for the congregational election of the clergy also has a striking similarity to an article of the German peasants, a continental influence on the rebels' thinking is indicated. Yet there are English precedents for the appeal to the Grand Manumission of Calvary in popular objections to serfdom. The source of the article remains obscure. By the sixteenth century, however, there were few Norfolk manors with bond families and when a new lessee in the Soke of Gimingham in 1552 tried to reimpose labour services and sued his tenants for nonperformance they said 'they hadde not donne the said works for the space of two hundreth yere'. The court said it was lawful for them to compound; labour services had retained a social stigma. The reference to the Grand Manumission of Calvary intruding upon this list of mundane economic grievances is a reminder of Kett's idealism. His religious articles seem to be inspired by a militant anticlericalism. But their overall purpose is the building of a more deeply religious and protestant society.

The hardships and discontents that made up the rebel programme were very diverse. Some, such as the request for fishing rights in article 19, were of purely local significance. This was fulfilled in a grant by charter of all fishes royal, as porpoises, grampuses and whales reserved to the crown by prerogative were called, made by Elizabeth to Yarmouth in 1559. The economic demands can be interpreted as the cry of the peasantry caught in the turmoil of the price revolution. But overall Kett's manifesto amounts to a comprehensive indictment of the exploitation by the Norfolk gentry of their dominant position in rural society. Kett's full purpose is manifest in article 27. Here his complaint was that the 'good lawes, statutes, proclamacons' of the Tudor governments had been deliberately disregarded by the Norfolk justices of the peace. He was protesting at the failure of the government to make the gentry enforce policies, such as that on enclosure, which were often against their interests. He expected Protector Somerset to give authority 'to suche comyssioners as your pore comons hath chosyn', or as he shall appoint, to remedy the situation which had come into being since 1485. He was so confident of the protector's support that he even asked him to make the offending officers of local government pay the commons a fair day's wage for each day they spent at Mousehold (article 28).

Kett did not regard himself as a rebel. Rather did he believe he was acting on the king's behalf and he tried to do everything in an ordered manner [**doc. 18**]. When the rebels combed the Norfolk villages to find sufficient food for the camp, they carried commissions signed by Kett and sent out in the king's name. 'John, of Great Yarmouth' was ordered to 'repair home and bring with you, with as much speed as may be, a last of beer, to maintain your poor neighbours withal, and if any man disturb or let you, in this business, he shall suffer imprisonment of body'.

The signatures of the representatives of twenty-two of the thirty-two Norfolk hundreds attached to the list of demands, provide some measure of the geographical basis of the rebellion. Men came to Mousehold from all over the county except from the Breckland, but it was strongly supported by those who lived along or near the road which pointed south through Wymondham and Attleborough. There was another strong concentration of rebels from the triangle of land between King's Lynn, East Dereham and Burnham and this accounts for the camp which was formed at Castle Rising. Lacking leadership of the calibre provided by Kett, this band of rebels moved south to Watton and Thetford, before joining the camp at Mousehold. One Suffolk hundred was represented among the signatures but the discontented there failed to coordinate the disturbances that took place throughout August. They were effectively suppressed by the local authorities. As the Breckland, a poor and thinly settled area not exposed to the same economic pressures as the rest of the county, contained most of the hundreds unrepresented, the area of the rebellion was in fact compact and self contained. From the Wash on the north-west to Yarmouth on the east coast it was sealed in by the sea.

There were forty-six gentry on the commission of the peace for Norfolk, yet only two made any attempt to prevent the formation of the camp at Mousehold. As far as possible they disregarded it throughout the anxious summer weeks until Warwick's army arrived. Faced with threats of being taken prisoner the gentry provided for the rebels' needs from their estates. This extraordinary situation came about because the trust between gentry and commons that made effective local government possible was lacking. The strongest impression left by the sources of Kett's rebellion is of the element of bitter class conflict that inspired it [**doc. 18**]. 'It were a good thing if there were so many gentlemen in Norfolk as there be white bulls' John Walker had said in 1540. 'As many as will not

75

turn to us, let us kill them, yea, even their children in the cradles', this troublemaker had urged. A Norfolk priest, canvassing support for the rebels in 1549 at Colchester, used violent propaganda about the behaviour of the gentry to awaken the interest of his hearers: 'that the gentlemen's servants of Lynn went abroad and killed poor men in their harvest work and also killed women there with child'.

The same sort of social tension existed in Norwich which, although it was the largest provincial city in the kingdom with a population of around 13,000 in 1549, lived in close contact with the surrounding countryside. A study of the trade structure of the city between 1525–75 has shown that its economy was coming to depend on the demands of the Norfolk gentry (**70**). As the textile trade declined more of the substantial families engaged in providing food, drink and household goods for local consumption. At the same time an integration of town and country developed as Norwich became fashionable as a social centre. The richer gentry began to divide their time between their town house and nearby estate.

The inequality of wealth in the city was very marked. About 6 per cent of the population owned approximately sixty per cent of the lands and goods. The subsidy assessment of 1525 shows that this group included the men whose viewpoint Sotherton represented: Aldrich, Steward, and Sotherton's father. While Thomas Aldrich was assessed in 1525 as worth £700 and was the second wealthiest man in the city, about 35 per cent of the citizens were too poor to pay even the minimum of fourpence. An attempt was made in the 1540s to provide new industries as the number of Norwich worsteds exported fell steadily. In 1543 the hatters became a separate company but it was inefficiently organised and the goods produced were of inadequate quality. By 1549 some craftsmen were emigrating; in May the Common Council complained that masons, carpenters, reeders and tilers were leaving to find work elsewhere. In their place 'foreigners' and beggars were invading the city. The ease with which Kett took control of Norwich is partly explained by the presence at a time of economic readjustment and instability of such dissolute elements, as well as by the material for social resentment that the city's economic structure provided.

Anger at social and economic inequality, especially when ostentatiously displayed, marks a number of the violent incidents of the rebellion; the killing of the Italian mercenary for instance and the treatment of the government's herald. 'How long shall we suffer this hireling doctor who being waged by Gentlemen is come hither with his tongue which is sold and tied to serve their appetites?' someone cried when Matthew Parker visited Mousehold. The rebels' distrust at once flared into open tumult and it was with difficulty that Kett's chaplain brought peace with the singing of the Te Deum while Parker hurriedly made his escape. Sotherton probably exaggerates such incidents as Mr Wharton's uncomfortable return to the city [**doc. 18**], but there is some other evidence to bear out the chroniclers' story of plunder and raiding. The Norwich City Chamberlain's accounts mention a payment for repairs 'in pecyng of ye dore stalle and dore loop of the tresyr howse which was sore hewyn and mankyld by traitor Ket and his Kytlyngs'.

Kett directed his demonstration against the provincial capital; it was the local situation which he was determined to remedy. The rebellion sprang from his misunderstanding of the government's attitude. It took all its energy from his outstanding leadership but it succeeded in the short term because the gentry's hold on the county was exceptionally weak. The Duke of Norfolk held predominant power in the county and owned over forty manors till the fall of his house in 1545. This was followed, as was the fall of his son in 1572, by bitter rivalries between county families and a scramble for lands (**78**). The factiousness of the county élite may have contributed to the lack of solidarity in the crisis of 1549. Moreover, the Bishop of Norwich from 1536–49, William Rugge, was a nonentity quite unfitted to give a lead in such a situation.

John Cheke, in his work of propaganda on behalf of the government *The Hurt of Sedition*, wrote scornfully of Kett's rebellion: 'ye pretende a commonwealth, how amende ye it by killynge of Gentlemen: by spoylynge of Gentilmen, by emprisonynge of Gentilmen?' He argued that it was the King's role to deal with gentry who misruled in the provinces: 'Thei rule but by law, if other wyse the law, the Counsayle, the King, breaketh their rule.' But Cheke did not understand the realities of the local situation. The commons of Norfolk were in rebellion because they were exasperated at the exploitation of the gentry. They chose the moment when they expected a sympathetic hearing in London.

7 Wyatt's Rebellion

CONSPIRACY AND REBELLION: NOVEMBER 1553–FEBRUARY 1554

In a petition of 16 November 1553, the House of Commons asked Queen Mary to marry within the realm. In her reply she made it clear that she was determined to stand by her decision to marry Philip of Spain. A conspiracy was then formed by a group of gentry who aimed to persuade Elizabeth to marry Edward Courtenay, a weak and unstable man who was a great-grandson of Edward IV. The intention was to put her on the throne in Mary's place. With sufficient support among the nobility and at court a political coup might have achieved this. When it was obvious that the Privy Council had accepted Mary's decision and such support was lacking, plans were made at the end of the year for a national and popular rising.

The leading conspirators were Sir James Croft, who had estates in Herefordshire, Sir Peter Carew and Sir Thomas Wyatt, of the Kentish gentry. All three of them had served Henry VIII in his French campaigns in the 1540s. Wyatt had been a member of the English council in France and Croft had been Lord Deputy of Ireland in 1551–2. Carew, having acted for Somerset against the Western Rebels in 1549, had sat as M.P. for Devonshire in 1553. The motives of these men were a mixture of self-interest and idealism. The idea of Spanish control of the court hurt their national pride. But their prospects of advancement were also at stake, since they depended on the court for further offices and rewards.

The rising was planned to take place on 18 March, just before Philip was due to start for England. The French were to provide naval support in the Channel and secure the south-western ports against the Spanish. Wyatt would hold the south-east against imperialist intervention from the Netherlands. A fourfold rising consisting of Croft from Herefordshire, Carew from Devon, Wyatt from Kent and the Duke of Suffolk from Leicestershire would converge on London.

The success of the rising depended on secrecy. In the counties it also depended on the energy and enthusiasm the gentry could inspire in the commons for a nebulous political cause. It was midwinter, the worst time to stir men from their homes, and there was no economic crisis to force them onto the road. Prices were much steadier than they had been in 1549. But scattered pieces of evidence suggest that in the west country at least there was spontaneous local feeling against the arrival of Philip. This seems to have sprung from wild rumours of Spanish intentions towards the country. At Christmas the French Ambassador heard that Plymouth was preparing to resist a Spanish landing. John Cowlyn, a Cornishman, had heard the rumour that 'before New Year's Day outlandish men will come upon our lands, for there be some at Plymouth already'.

In early January news of the conspiracy was leaking out. Simon Renard, the imperial ambassador and leader of the Spanish faction, knew of it. He was suspicious of the failure of Carew to appear before the Council when summoned, and told the Queen as much as he knew. The conspirators hoped to retain the initiative by acting at once. Wyatt had left the capital when, on 21 January, Gardiner, the Lord Chancellor, managed to worm the gist of the plot out of the foolish and unreliable Courtenay.

Abortive risings followed in the west and the midlands. Croft, caught out by the speed with which events had moved, never attempted to raise Herefordshire. The Duke of Suffolk found little support for his cause at Leicester where, in Holinshed's words, 'few there were that would willingly hearken' to his proclamation against the Spanish marriage. While Leicester was apathetic, Coventry was hostile. Holinshed relates how the people there 'had put themselves in armour and made all provision they could to defend the city against the said Duke'. When Suffolk heard this news he gave up. He went into hiding but was found and arrested two days later by the Earl of Huntingdon, who the government had sent north after him. He was escorted to London by the Earl and 300 horse. It was only a week since Suffolk had left London and he had never gathered round him more than about 140 men, most of whom were his own retainers. The Spanish were too obscure and distant a threat to midland gentry, townsmen and peasants.

Sir Peter Carew had reached his Devon home before Christmas

and, in his anxiety to raise support for his cause, made little effort to conceal his plans. His anti-Spanish propaganda gained him the help of a few extreme protestant gentry but no group of substantial and influential men joined him. For the most part he seems merely to have caused rumour and alarm. The sheriff, Sir Thomas Denys, was determined to safeguard the county from rebellion and retained the confidence of most of the gentry. Carew lacked sufficient influence to carry the county behind him. The commons remembered too well his suppression of the 1549 rebellion. The Devon gentry were regarded as a class apart. They had acted with the government in 1549 and were associated in the popular mind with the protestant régimes of Somerset and Northumberland.

So it was Carew's own servants who paraded a waggon-load of armour through Exeter and prepared to defend his manor at Mohun's Ottery, near Honiton. Meanwhile Sir Thomas Denys was active in garrisoning Exeter against attack. Carew began to see that with such insubstantial support his chances of seizing and holding the county town as a demonstration, or organising a force to march on London, were very small. He became convinced he was about to be arrested and on 25 January abandoned the rising and sailed for the safety of Normandy. The rising in the west had failed before Wyatt had even assembled his army at Rochester.

The crown always had reason to be sensitive to the rise of powerful families in Kent, strategically placed as it was between London and the continent. Partly for reasons of security, they tended to reward their servants and administrators with lands there. Sir Thomas Wyatt came of a family who had served the first two Tudors loyally. The Kentish estates he inherited in 1542 made him one of the largest landowners in the county. He was well placed to act as a local leader since from 1550, when he was sheriff of the county, he had taken a particular interest in the defence of Kent and of the Edwardian regime against disorder and unrest. Alarmed by the rebellions of 1549 he had drawn up a scheme to protect the government in time of crisis by a handpicked militia [**doc. 20**]. Wyatt took a keen interest in military matters and wrote a formal treatise on the militia. His leadership of his own organisation helped him to collect a force quickly when the need arose in January 1554. His success in this, compared with the dismal failure of Carew and Suffolk, was remarkable. Arriving home at Allington Castle, near Maidstone on 19 January he spent the next few days coordinating his plans with the small group of his friends whose help he knew he could count on. The government was uncertain of the connection between the news they heard of unrest in Devon and in Kent, but they were bound to treat as serious a threat of disturbance so near the capital, when there was no army to defend it. They sent a herald to Allington with an offer of negotiations, though there was never a chance of Mary meeting the rebels' grievances. Wyatt dismissed him. On 25 January he raised his standard at Maidstone and proclamations were simultaneously issued there and in other towns. Wyatt then set up his headquarters at Rochester, where by 27 January he had collected a force of around 2,000 men. Further forces had gathered at Tonbridge and Sevenoaks. It was then only just over a week since Wyatt had come home.

John Proctor relates how the rebel leader went about his highly effective anti-Spanish propaganda. His main theme was the immediate danger to the realm of Spanish control. He dramatised the arrival a few weeks before of the emperor's envoys for the marriage treaty:

> lo, now even at hand Spaniards be now already arrived at Dover, at one passage to the number of a hundred, passing upward to London, in companies of ten, four and six, with harness, harquebuses, and morions, with matchlight, the foremost company where of be already at Rochester.

The danger was made to seem local and immediate.

Wyatt appealed to the men's patriotism. 'Because you be our friends and because you be Englishmen that you will join with us, as we will with you unto death, in this behalf; protesting unto you before God . . . we seek no harm to the Queen, but better counsel and councillors.' He was clever enough to unite moderates and radicals in his cause. 'You may not so much as name religion, for that will withdraw from us the hearts of many', he warned a protestant supporter. To a doubter who asked 'Sir is your quarrel only to defend us from overrunning by Strangers?' he replied: 'We mind nothing less than any wise to touch her Grace.' Like other rebel leaders, Wyatt allayed the fears and consciences of many by posing as the rescuer of the Queen from foolish advice. He concealed from the majority that he aimed at the deposition of the Queen; Proctor relates that when he revealed his true intentions at Rochester to those of his captains who were not already in his confidence some of them 'wished themselves under the earth for being so unhappy as to be so much as acquainted with so damnable an enterprise'.

But by then Wyatt's propaganda had been sufficiently decisive to ensure that many of the gentry who did not join the rebels at least sympathised with them sufficiently to be unwilling to oppose them. In these circumstances the most active royalists, Sir Robert Southwell, the sheriff, and Lord Abergavenny found it difficult to raise forces in the county. On 28 January they took up a position at Malling with about 600 men. Here they were well placed to intercept Sir Henry Isley who set out that day from Sevenoaks to join Wyatt at Rochester. Isley had about 500 men. The two forces met near Wrotham and after a fierce skirmish Isley's men fled the field, leaving the sheriff sixty prisoners. The news of this setback reached Wyatt about the same time as he heard that the royal force of Whitecoats, consisting of 500 hastily mustered Londoners under the Duke of Norfolk, had arrived at Gravesend. Norfolk was now over eighty and past his prime as a military leader. He failed to make contact with Southwell and ignored the warnings of Lord Cobham, who had collected 300 loyalists to join him at Gravesend, that the Londoners were not trustworthy. Their disloyalty was dramatically proved when they came down the hill to Rochester shouting 'We are all Englishmen' and, according to a prearranged plan, deserted to the rebels. Norfolk retreated to London and the Tower chronicler describes the tattered arrival of his few remaining men: 'You should have seen some of the guard come home, their coats turned and all ruined, without arrows or string in their bow, or sword, in very strange wise.'

Wyatt now had a magnificent opportunity. He had been able to seize some of the Queen's ships ready in the river below Gravesend for the escort of her bridegroom, and some cannon as well. His forces had grown to about 3,000 and the Whitecoats urged him to make a rapid advance: 'London', they said, 'longed sore for their coming.' Everything now depended on the attitude of the city and this still lay in the balance.

The Whitecoats desertion suggested that Wyatt had a real chance of gaining the sympathy and active support of the capital. But he moved too slowly. Leaving Rochester on 30 January he wasted time in an assault on Lord Cobham at Cooling Castle. Cobham was captured and a day lost. On the 31st the government repeated their offer to Wyatt. The Council had rejected Renard's suggestion of an appeal for troops to the Emperor and the Queen still had no adequate military forces. Despite this the offer of a committee to discuss grievances arising out of the marriage settlement and a pardon to all those who returned home at once was not in fact sincere. It was a blind while the Queen prepared her defences; it answered her purpose in that Wyatt was delayed at Blackheath. When in his reply he demanded the custody of the Tower and the Queen as a hostage as security for an agreement, any chance of peaceful settlement was finally ended.

Mary rose to the occasion. Proclaiming Wyatt and his company 'rank traitors' she made a rousing and successful appeal to the citizens of London for their loyalty. She was convinced that her enemies must be heretics; that, as she told them, 'the matter of the marriage seemed to be but a Spanish cloak to cover their pretended purpose against our religion'. She was unscrupulous in claiming that she would follow parliament's advice on her marriage. Then she appealed to their hearts: 'Certainly if a prince and governor may as naturally and earnestly love her subjects as the mother doth love the child, then assure yourselves that I, being your lady and mistress, do as earnestly and tenderly love and favour you.' Here Mary showed some of the Tudor skill in flattery of which her sister Elizabeth was to make such good use. After the cheers and demonstrations of loyalty that followed her speech at the Guildhall she felt secure enough to trust herself to the citizens and the forces the Earl of Pembroke was raising, and her determination not to leave the city grew. By the time Wyatt arrived at Southwark on the morning of 3 February there were 'men in harness night and day' guarding every gate, and, more important, London Bridge was held against the rebels.

At Southwark however, as the chronicler relates, the rebels 'were suffered peaceably to enter and the said inhabitants most willingly with their best entertained them'. They waited there three days uncertain what to do next. Apart from looting the palace and library of the Bishop of Winchester, they remained orderly throughout. Wyatt still hoped for support within the city. He realised it was important to maintain a reputation for good behaviour.

On 6 February Wyatt suddenly left Southwark and marched to Kingston. Thirty feet of the bridge there had been broken down but his men rigged it up sufficiently to take them and the cannon across. It was ten o'clock at night when the rebels started their march back along the north bank to surprise the city, still hoping friends might open the gates to them. On the way the carriage of one of the great guns broke down and precious time was lost before Wyatt was persuaded to abandon it. When they reached Knightsbridge before dawn the next morning they were hungry and weary and the Earl of Pembroke's force was already drawn up above St James's.

The Londoners were out early and ready to defend the city but their behaviour, as Wyatt with a dwindling force came on from Knightsbridge to Ludgate, was strangely unlike the resistance of loyal subjects to a band of rebels. There must have been considerable sympathy for Wyatt and his cause, because it seems likely that the reason why Pembroke's men did not attack until Wyatt was past was that Pembroke could not control them. And some of the citizens lining Fleet Street even drew back to let Wyatt pass [**doc. 21**]. It may be that the rebels' cries that the Queen had granted their requests and pardoned them were believed.

As Wyatt approached Ludgate the mood of the populace remained indecisive but there the gate was closed. He knew then that he was defeated. The wavering confidence of the people now came down on the side of the government. Some of those who had watched Wyatt advance attacked him as he retreated. The rebel leader soon surrendered and the small band of 300 who had kept with him till the end put up little resistance. About forty people were killed.

The government had survived, but there was no agreement in the Council on a coherent policy of punishment which might ensure the stability of the regime. Mary convinced herself that her fragile victory meant she had the country's support and that it would be strengthened by the return to orthodoxy and Rome that she longed for. Gardiner, reading the rebellion along the same religious lines, believed that the only safe course was the extermination of heresy. But Philip, when he arrived, opposed this. Renard pressed the Queen to rid herself of Courtenay and Elizabeth, the obvious rallying points for further discontent. He saw no safety for Philip in England with them still alive. Elizabeth was held prisoner in the Tower for some weeks, but no evidence could be found to incriminate her (**24,** p. 44). In her speech to parliament on the succession in 1566, she made it clear that she had not been ignorant of the practices against her sister, but hinted that she had disapproved of them (**25,** vol. 1 p. 148).

Mary as usual was the victim of confusing advice but Lord Paget, whose faction had gained considerably in influence from the defeat of Wyatt, had the bulk of influential opinion behind him in advocating leniency. No punitive campaign like that of 1497 or 1536 followed the rebellion. A number of the conspirators were charged with levying war against the queen, but only two were brought to trial. One was acquitted and the other was pardoned after a period of imprisonment.

With public opinion so strongly against severity it was sensible for the government to be lenient. By the end of February about 480 of those who took part in the rebellion had been convicted, but the vast majority were pardoned at once or after a period of imprisonment. Six hundred men who were in custody were brought before the Queen 'coupled together two and three, a rope running between them'. After she had pardoned them they were released, to the rejoicing of the city. Under a hundred executions took place and they were not distributed in an even way to overawe the people of Kent. The Kentish men lost less than thirty out of 350 convicted, eight or nine of whom were gentry. The Londoners suffered more heavily, losing forty-five out of the seventy-six convicted. Wyatt himself went to the block on 11 April and the French Ambassador reported that the people pressed to dip their handkerchiefs in his blood. His legend was quickly being established.

THE REBELLION AND THE SPANISH MARRIAGE

The conspiracy of 1553 to depose the queen arose because of the ineffectiveness of the constitutional methods of opposition to the royal marriage policy. Mary was exercising her rightful prerogative when she expressed her annoyance at the commons' petition in November 1553 and told them 'she found it very strange' that they should interfere in such a personal matter; for 'to force her to take a husband who would not be to her liking would be to cause her death'. The rebellion was merely a more dramatic and violent phase in the agitation against the Spanish marriage that had grown since Mary's intentions became clear earlier in the autumn.

The rising in the midlands was ineptly executed and that in the west was inadequately based. Only in Kent, where it was a rising of the gentry, was the issue sufficiently immediate and the leadership sufficiently capable to make success possible. The support of the commons depended entirely on their leadership. As the map of recorded participants in the rebellion on pages 88–9 shows, the strongest contingents came from parishes where there was a gentleman who supported Wyatt. He had the loyalty of a number of influential gentry in the central and western part of the county but hardly any support in the east, which remained largely unaffected by the rebellion. Men like Sir Henry Isley, Sir George Harper and Thomas Culpepper had been closely associated with Wyatt in the government of the county during Edward VI's reign. Each of these men had been sheriff in the years 1548–52 and a family like the Culpeppers, long established in Kent, enjoyed a network of family connections.

The rising sprang much more from fears and exaggerated rumours of what Philip might do than any firm evidence of his intentions when he became Mary's husband. It was feared that Philip would dominate the court and government and involve the country in the European conflict, with the heavy expenditure this would entail. Such a prospect alarmed the landlord and parliamentary classes who disliked paying subsidies. The Habsburg grip might be strengthened if there were a child of the marriage, or if childbearing proved fatal. The marriage treaty prepared by the Privy Council and signed on 12 January 1554 in theory safeguarded the country's laws and customs. Only Englishmen were to fill offices in church and state. If Mary died childless, all Philip's rights in England would die with her.

But there was no way people could be sure Philip would keep his promises. And in fact when he first heard the terms of the treaty he registered a secret protest that he would not consider himself absolutely bound by them. Yet there is no evidence that Philip intended through the marriage to try to impose on England a more centralised administration on the Spanish pattern, such as might have weakened or excluded the local power of the gentry, or that he even wanted to rule the country himself. His brief experience of England made him unwilling to come back. The purpose of the marriage from Philip's point of view is more likely to have been primarily dynastic. The Emperor Charles V had been attracted by its diplomatic possibilities in the great struggle of Habsburg and Valois. It was too obvious a move in the game of power politics for a skilled and opportunistic player to miss. Its impact on English politics was complicated by fears of the implications that the personal inadequacy and political incompetence of Mary suggested.

Her distrust of her people was well known, and increased the suspicions of the gentry. Girolamo Soranzo wrote that she scorned to be English and boasted her Spanish blood.

D. M. Loades in his recent study of the conspiracy came to the conclusion that 'the real reasons which lay behind it were secular and political' (**18**). The evidence available about the religious leanings of the leaders is certainly inconclusive, but not entirely without weight. Carew had a reputation for protestantism in the west and was indicted in 1554 *'impie et erronie religionis'*. Croft, the ringleader, had been responsible for introducing the protestant liturgy to Ireland in 1551. The Duke of Suffolk had entertained the Swiss reformer Bullinger when he visited England and seems to have been a sincere protestant. There is no reason on the other hand to think that Sir Thomas Wyatt was inspired by devotion to protestantism. He repudiated any such motive in public and the defence of his actions written in the 1590s by a close friend emphasised that 'religion was not the cause of his rising'. Yet this defence perhaps exaggerated the patriotic aims of the conspiracy as anti-Spanish propaganda (**94**).

There is some evidence of religious extremism, including anti-trinitarianism, among the Kentish commons in the area around Tonbridge, Maidstone and Cranbrook, and there was certainly a strong protestant tradition in Maidstone. A radical pressure group had been active in the town since at least 1547. It had been in correspondence with Bullinger and there were contacts with the very energetic Bocking protestants of Essex. One of the leaders of this group had already gone into exile by 1554 but another, William Smith, a yeoman, was before the Privy Council for distributing heretical literature only a few weeks before the rising took place. Smith himself was among the rebels whose fines were recorded in the Exchequer, and Maidstone provided by far the largest number of recorded participants in the rising. While seventy-eight Maidstone men are recorded, the next largest contingent, Smarden, provided only thirty-two.

We lack the evidence to chart the other grievances and discontents which, although irrelevant to the Spanish marriage, may have led particular individuals to follow Wyatt. The largest contingent with no gentry leader came from Cranbrook, the centre of the Wealden cloth industry. Those of them who were clothworkers by trade may have been more ready to rebel because of unemploy-

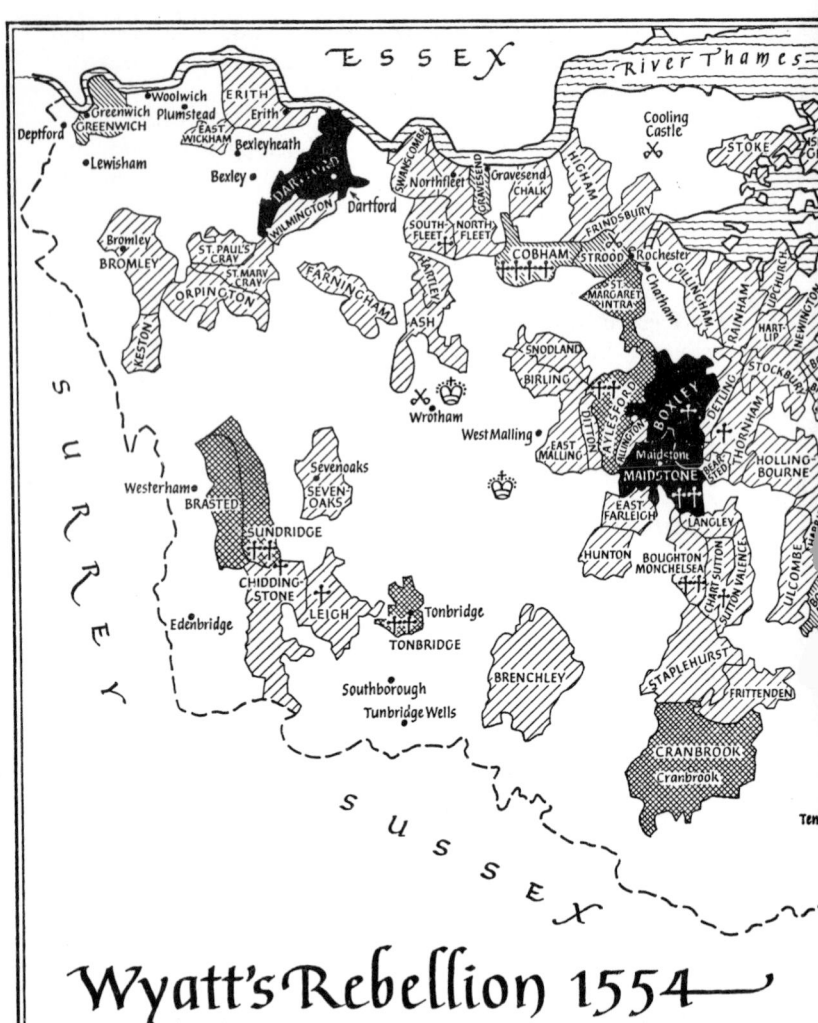

Wyatt's Rebellion 1554

Map of Kent showing distribution of recorded participants in Wyatt's rising (by parishes). The parishes shown are taken from the first survey of civil parishes, begun in 1838, and approximate closely to the original ecclesiastical parishes.

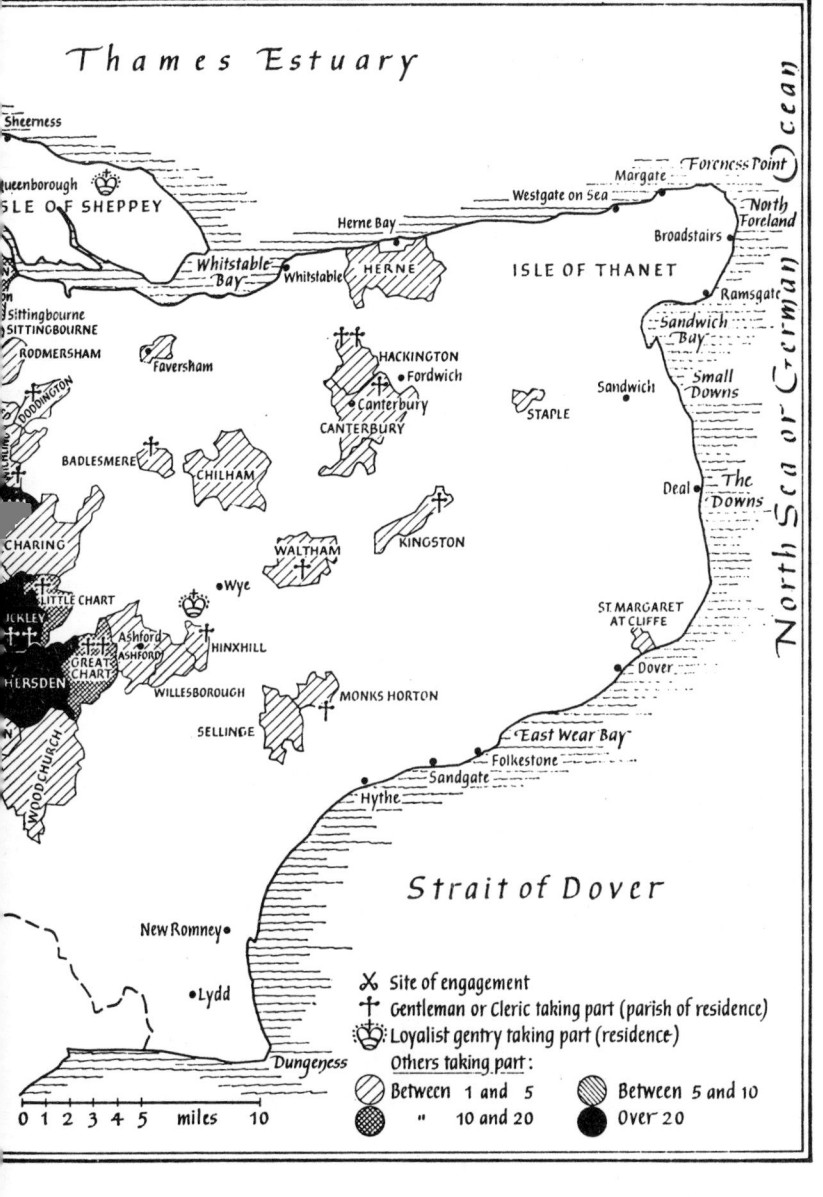

Thames Estuary

Sheerness
Queenborough
ISLE OF SHEPPEY
Sittingbourne
SITTINGBOURNE
RODMERSHAM
Faversham
DODDINGTON
BADLESMERE
CHILHAM
CHARING
LITTLE CHART
UCKLEY
Ashford
ASHFORD
GREAT CHART
HERSDEN
Wye
HINXHILL
WILLESBOROUGH
SELLINGE
WOODCHURCH

Whitstable Bay
Whitstable
HERNE
Herne Bay
Westgate on Sea
Margate
Foreness Point
North Foreland
Broadstairs
ISLE OF THANET
Ramsgate
Sandwich Bay
Small Downs
HACKINGTON
Fordwich
Canterbury
CANTERBURY
STAPLE
Sandwich
WALTHAM
KINGSTON
Deal
The Downs
ST. MARGARET AT CLIFFE
MONKS HORTON
East Wear Bay
Folkestone
Sandgate
Hythe
Dover

North Sea or German Ocean

Strait of Dover

New Romney
Lydd
Dungeness

0 1 2 3 4 5   miles   10

✗ Site of engagement
✝ Gentleman or Cleric taking part (parish of residence)
♛ Loyalist gentry taking part (residence)
Others taking part :
◯ Between 1 and 5   ◯ Between 5 and 10
● "   10 and 20   ● Over 20

ment following the depression in the cloth trade since 1551. But it is impossible to impose any pattern of economic causation. Over thirty different trades are represented among the recorded rebels and no one group predominated. Any attempt to explain the rebellion in terms of vested interests, or 'ins' against 'outs', also breaks down. The backgrounds of rebel and royalist gentry were very similar. Both Wyatt and Southwell, for instance, had benefited from the sale of Kentish monastic lands.

The foundation of Tudor authority was the dynasty's hold on the confidence of London and the south east. This confidence had been weakened by unpopular war taxation in 1525. In 1554 it was at stake. The Londoners' attitude at Rochester showed that Mary temporarily had lost it. Their detachment when the rebels marched into London meant that Mary's survival was a close thing. Wyatt came nearer than any other Tudor rebel to toppling a monarch from the throne.

Yet in the political development of the century the significance of the rebellion is that it failed. This demonstrated the bankruptcy of rebellion as a way of solving this kind of political crisis. The critical issue posed by the Spanish marriage was the question as to who should rule. It appeared that the only sanction, if either Philip or Mary broke the terms of the marriage treaty, was rebellion. This was a weapon that, after the social disorders of 1549, few were prepared to risk using. So the gentry learnt to channel their opposition through parliament (**25,** vol. 1). They prevented Philip's coronation and frustrated Mary's plans to disinherit Elizabeth by statute. Wyatt's rebellion has recently been interpreted as 'an attempt to join in the debate about what foreign policy should be' (**45**). If the evidence of the rebels' religious motivations is indecisive it at least deserves more serious consideration. Foreign policy, marriage and religion were all to be important causes of conflict between Elizabeth and her parliaments; they were also the issues which caused the crisis of the reign of Mary.

8 The Northern Rebellion

CONSPIRACY AND REBELLION 1569-70

The arrival of Mary, Queen of Scots, in England in 1568 led to a long series of conspiracies centring round her person. The first complex of these, overlapping in purpose but disconnected, was developed in the tense atmosphere of the spring and summer of 1569 when the fracas arising from the seizure of Philip II's bullion ships, a landmark in the breaking of Spanish amity, coincided with a critical situation in the politics of the Elizabethan court. At the end of a decade of Elizabethan government, protestantism had not yet taken a hold on the country and the question of the succession remained open and disturbing. In the intrigues and schemes of this year it is necessary to disentangle the roles of the protagonist, Mary, and of two groups of nobles—those at court who disliked the prestige and policies of Cecil, and the catholic earls in the north.

When Mary crossed the border as a deposed queen she came expecting support in the north. Three years before she had told a catholic priest that she 'trusted to find many friends when time did serve, especially among those of the old religion'. Among those who paid court to the exiled queen at Carlisle was Thomas Percy, seventh Earl of Northumberland. During the months of her captivity which followed Mary exchanged letters with the earl and encouraged his loyalty by sending him and his wife rings and tokens. Northumberland was in sympathy with a group of his friend's efforts to' release Mary from Wingfield in the summer of 1569. They failed because of the difficulty of obtaining cooperation within the house.

Mary's future had rapidly become the catalyst of court politics in 1568-9 (**24,** chapters 10 and 11). The plan for a marriage between the Duke of Norfolk and the Scottish Queen made him the central figure in a conspiracy that gained the support of a group of substantial nobility (**46,** chapters 8 and 9). The match was suggested to Norfolk by Secretary Maitland, one of the Scottish regent Murray's commissioners, at the conference held at York in October 1568 to try to settle Mary's future. It was taken up by protestants such as Leicester and Throckmorton, as a sensible solution to two related problems: what to do about Mary and the succession. By early 1569 it had become part of a court intrigue to overthrow Cecil, who seemed to the more conservative nobles like Arundell and Pembroke to be leading England too close to a confrontation with the Catholic powers. The Norfolk–Mary marriage would enable the Queen to settle the succession and make a lasting peace with France and Spain.

But Elizabeth was not interested in settling the succession and refused to consider letting her leading nobleman marry the most dangerous claimant to her throne. Furthermore she dealt firmly with Leicester's attack on Cecil for mishandling policy in February 1569. After this the court conspirators delayed broaching their plans to Elizabeth throughout the spring and summer because they were afraid of her answer. They hoped that Murray would do it for them as part of the negotiations for Mary's restoration to the Scottish throne. But, late in July, Murray decided against Mary's restoration on any terms. Norfolk spent the summer progress during August in an agony of indecision. He lacked the courage to be open with the queen who was by now well aware of the rumoured marriage. Finally on 6 September Leicester confessed. Ten days later Norfolk found he could bear the atmosphere of suspicion and rumour no longer and left the court without leave. When, afraid to obey Elizabeth's summons to Windsor, the duke then left London for his home at Kenninghall in Norfolk, it was assumed that he had gone to raise the north. Elizabeth, expecting a general rising, quickly took precautions to ensure that Mary's captivity was secure.

There is no evidence that any coherent plan for a rebellion in the north did in fact exist at this stage. Certainly Mary had been tireless in her letters of encouragement to all whose help she hoped for both in England and abroad. Certainly Ridolfi had been active in maintaining contact between the southern nobility and the Papacy and de Spes had regularly written to Philip II in wildly optimistic terms about the success of the rebellion. But until almost the last moment the weakest link was the Earl of Northumberland. His resistance to the marriage plan coloured his negotiations with both

Mary and de Spes. He had told Mary 'how her marriage with the Duke was disliked he being counted a Protestant, and if she looked to recover her estate, it must be by advancing the Catholic religion'. He had suggested to de Spes that Mary might marry Philip of Spain but had found the ambassador uncommunicative; he suspected 'from my small affection to the Queen of Scots marriage with the Duke'. There is no reason to doubt Northumberland's own account: he was prepared to bring his tenantry to the support of a Catholic rising but he never intended 'to hazard myself for the marriage' [**doc. 24**]. The court conspiracy and the northern rebellion were only tenuously linked; the uncertainty and confusion when Elizabeth outwitted the former provided just sufficient encouragement to activate the latter.

Back in his own country Norfolk's nerve failed him. Instead of raising his East Anglian tenantry he spent a week of indecision. He gave no firm lead to the faint-hearted local gentry. Then on 1 October, sending a message north to the Earl of Westmoreland, his brother-in-law, telling him not to rise, he set out for London to throw himself on Elizabeth's mercy. Within a fortnight he was in the Tower.

The north had been full of rumours that August and September, spread, as Sir George Bowes later reported, 'by the assemble and conference of people at fares'. There were rumours of the Norfolk–Mary marriage and their succession and there was 'the bruit of altering religion'. The earls had read Norfolk's withdrawal from court as a signal for action and turned from vague scheming to more deliberate planning. The duke's sudden and unexpected capitulation, at the moment when all their hopes had been built on his support and cooperation in the south, forced them to abandon the rising fixed for 6 October. The north was left aroused and confused. News of the abortive rising inevitably reached the Earl of Sussex, who as President of the Council of the North was responsible for the security of the northern counties. The month before the earls and 'all the principal gentlemen and their wives of this country' had been staying with him and hunting at Cawood near York. Though incredulous of the rumours he now heard, he was forced to treat the earls as potential rebels. Sussex knew that because of his friendship with Norfolk his loyalty was already in doubt at court. In his letters at this time he was anxious to emphasise his activity in enquiring into rumours of sedition.

On 9 October the two earls appeared before the Council of the North at York. They agreed that they had heard the same rumours as Sussex but maintained disingenuously that they did not know their origin. They even said they would 'make diligent enquiry for the first authors'. Sussex accepted their word but reported to the Privy Council that he had plans ready to take York, Hull, Pontefract and Knaresborough if there were a rebellion. In Yorkshire control of these towns was crucial in an open conflict just as further north control of the country depended on holding the strongholds of such places as Barnard, Brancepeth, Alnwick and Naworth (Map 4, p. 97). But on 13 October Sussex was confident enough to report 'all is very quiet here and the time of year will shortly cool hot humours'.

Elizabeth was not satisfied about the loyalty of either the Earls or Sussex himself. On 24 October she demanded full accounts of the 'bruits' from all the members of the Council of the North; the earls were to be summoned to court. New and disturbing stories were by now reaching Sussex, that a large meeting was planned at Northumberland's estate at Topcliffe, where he was then staying, and that he, as the only man who threatened the earl's design to control the northern counties, would be the first taken. Northumberland himself in fact remained hesitant at this time and had received discouraging replies from Mary and de Spes about the chances of a rebellion succeeding [**doc. 24**]. Even the local gentry had 'answered coldly'. But by the first week in November the Neville tenantry were flocking in to the Earl of Westmoreland's castle at Brancepeth, while those gentry who were determined to remain loyal were gathering round Sir George Bowes at Barnard Castle. Durham was in a turmoil as men suddenly found themselves caught in the crosscurrents of bastard feudal and national loyalties. Their instinct in such a situation was to move to the safety of towns and castles.

Sussex rightly feared that the summons to the earls would force them into open rebellion, but he had to carry out the Queen's commands. Towards midnight on 9 November his messenger, about to leave Topcliffe, heard the church bells ring backwards as the signal to raise the county. Northumberland had been forced into activity by his more enthusiastic followers who made him believe a force had come to take him. He went to Brancepeth where he was persuaded to join the rebellion [**doc. 24**].

By 13 November Sussex was sending out commissions for raising forces against the earls. He hoped to collect 1,500 footmen at Darlington by 21 November but he was to be sorely disappointed in this. Sir George Bowes's almost daily reports to Sussex from Barnard Castle provided him with a dismal account of the state of the bishopric. It was effectively in the control of the earls and the 300 of their men who had already come in to Brancepeth. Their mounted tenantry terrified the neighbourhood, threatening to spoil any gentry who would not join them: 'They passe in troppes, armed and unarmed, so fast up and down the contrethe that no man dare well stirre anywhere.' Despite all this activity disagreement continued among the leaders and there does not seem even now to have been a clear plan of campaign. Bowes heard rumours they might go north to Alnwick or Holy Island and that there was 'shippe ready to pass away', a story in fact without foundation. On 7 November he had written to Sussex: 'Sewre I take this assembly to be more done for fear, than there ys any evil pretendyt to be done.' He continued to think the earls' purpose was more 'theire owne saifety than to annoye'.

On 14 November the earls made their first demonstration, marching to Durham Cathedral where they tore down all evidences of protestantism and celebrated mass. They returned to Brancepeth for the night but the next day began a march south which they continued till they reached Bramham Moor near Tadcaster a week later. Their progress was slow because they stopped to make proclamations and raise the North Riding on the way [**doc. 22**]. Durham was the heart of the rebellion: the cathedral had acted as a focus for its emotions and the bishopric provided 794 of the recorded participants. But large numbers also joined the rising from Richmondshire when their support was demanded with promises of money and under the threat of spoil and burning. Away from their own estates the earls were ready to force the commons to join them. Bowes says that most of the 'poore rascall footemen' were 'unarmed and brought forwards by coercion'. Further additions to the rebels' strength resulted from Christopher Neville's diversion east to raise the Earl of Westmoreland's tenants around Kirby Moorside, where he 'threw down the communion board' as the earls had done at Durham.

Sussex, who had only 400 ill-equipped horsemen, dared not leave York and face the rebels in the field. On 16 November he had written bitterly to the Privy Council of his difficulties in levying men: 'Every man seeks to bring as small a force as he can of horsemen and the footmen find fault with the weather.' On 22 November the rebels paused for two days at Bramham Moor. At their musters there they had 3,800 footmen, mostly 'artificers and the meanest sort of husbandmen', and 1,600 horsemen. It was in the horsemen that their real strength lay: they were, according to Bowes, 'for the most part gentlemen and their household servants and tenants and the head husbandmen'.

For a short time the country around York was paralysed by the rebels' presence. A vanguard of horseman patrolled the Ouse. Sussex stopped sending letters to London for fear they would be intercepted. Lord Hunsdon, coming south to assist Sussex from Newcastle, cautiously approached York by way of Hull. All the country east of the Pennines was at this time at the earl's command. 'All things are here out of order and my dealing and good wyll can not amende yt', wrote Bowes in despair on 23 November. Yet on the 24 November the rebels turned back to Knaresborough.

Why at this point did their resolution crack? They may have feared the rumours of the massive force being organised in the south by the Earl of Warwick and the Lord Admiral Clinton or have known that Hunsdon had sent a message warning Cecil to move Mary from Tutbury. However serious they had been in their intention to reach Mary and release her, they now abandoned the plan. It depended on the support of Lancashire and Cheshire and this had not been forthcoming. In fact the appeals the earls had made to the Catholic nobility had failed completely. Beyond the Aire and the Don was unknown country, a land where the names of Neville and Norton meant little, and a land more firmly linked to the capital by the tentacles of Elizabethan government. At Bramham the rebel leaders realised their weakness outside the north and their nerve failed. As they turned again towards their own estates the wavering and uncertain country at their backs began to doubt and distrust them.

Once the retreat had begun the rebels did not stop until they reached Brancepeth on 30 November. Meanwhile Sussex found the tide of loyalty turning in his favour. 'The soldiers wax more trusty', he reported to Cecil on 26 November: He began to speak of the rebels as men with 'their hearts broken'. But a desperate lack of armour and horsemen still detained him in York. The southern army was slow in coming north and with 10,000 men was unnecessarily large and expensive anyway, as Sussex and Hunsdon continually

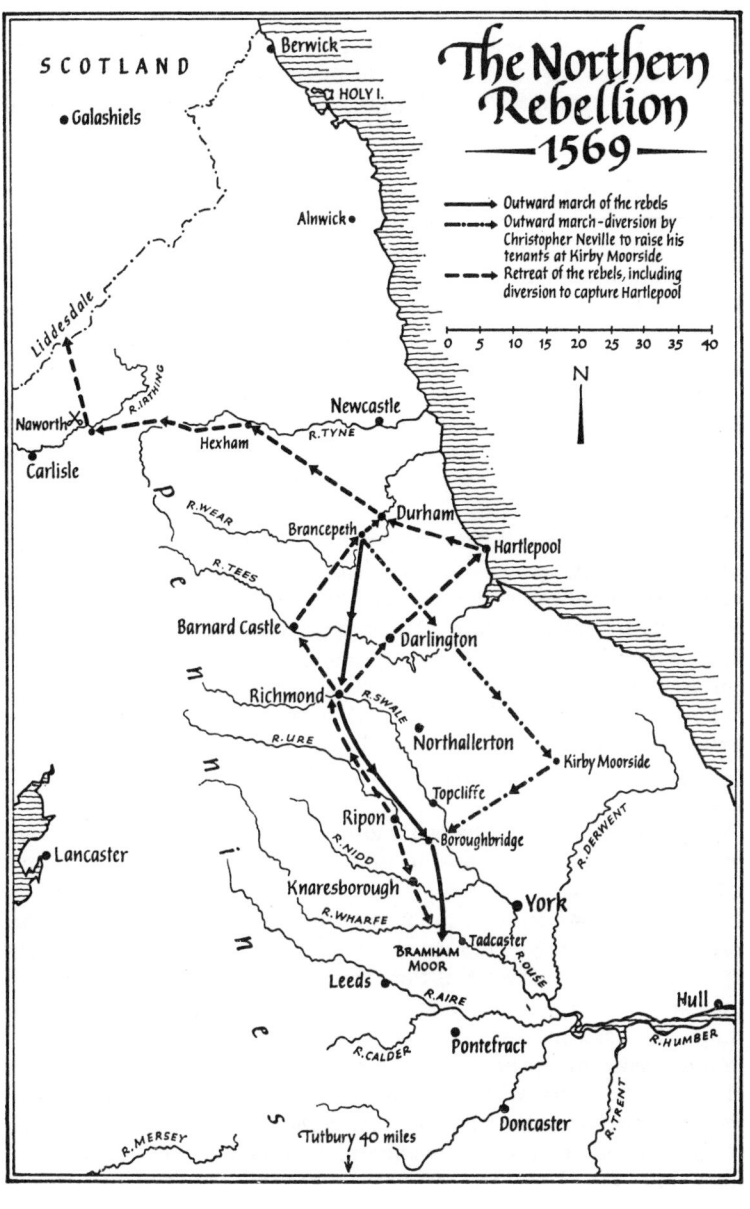

The Northern Rebellion —1569—

SCOTLAND

- Galashiels
- Berwick
- HOLY I.
- Alnwick

→ Outward march of the rebels
⊸⊸⊸ Outward march – diversion by Christopher Neville to raise his tenants at Kirby Moorside
⊸ ⊸ ⊸ Retreat of the rebels, including diversion to capture Hartlepool

0 5 10 15 20 25 30 35 40

N

Liddesdale

R. IRTHING

Newcastle

R. TYNE

Naworth

Hexham

Carlisle

R. WEAR

Durham

Brancepeth

Hartlepool

R. TEES

P
e
n
n
i
n
e
s

Barnard Castle

Darlington

Richmond

R. SWALE

R. URE

Northallerton

Kirby Moorside

Topcliffe

R. DERWENT

Ripon

R. NIDD

Boroughbridge

Lancaster

Knaresborough

R. WHARFE

York

Tadcaster

R. OUSE

BRAMHAM MOOR

Leeds

R. AIRE

Hull

R. HUMBER

R. CALDER

Pontefract

R. TRENT

R. MERSEY

Tutbury 40 miles

Doncaster

pointed out to Cecil. In vain they pressed the government for 500 horse and 300 shot that they might pursue the rebels, but the Lord Admiral, writing from Lincolnshire, could only offer 100 horsemen.

Although some of the rebel footmen, 'who were promised wages and not paid', deserted and went home on the way through Yorkshire and Durham, 3,200 foot and 1,500 horse came to besiege Sir George Bowes in Barnard Castle in the first week of December. Meanwhile a contingent went and took Hartlepool, hoping that Spanish troops might land there to help them. But Northumberland later said that the message promising Spanish support was very likely a ruse by Richard Norton, the veteran rebel of 1536, to encourage them. The earls had certainly not maintained regular contact with any foreign powers. Philip II's attitude in his letters to de Spes had never been more than lukewarm and Alva showed no interest in the conspiracy. The Spanish king was hardly likely to be enthusiastic about a plan to put Mary on the throne because of her Guise connection.

On 14 December Bowes reported to Cecil how, with the castle near starvation, 226 of his men had leaped the walls to join the rebels. He had been delivered into their hands by another 150 who 'suddenly set open the gate'. The siege was a burst of revenge on the man who had stood most firmly against the rebels in their own country and whose demesnes and crops they had already destroyed. When Bowes surrendered he was allowed to depart into Yorkshire with 400 men. He ended his letter to Cecil with one of those moving protestations of loyalty which Elizabeth so frequently inspired: 'I have nothing but my horse, armour and weapons brought out from Barnard castle, which I more esteem than twenty times as much of other things, because thereby I am enabled to serve my good Queen.'

On 16 December, with the royal army at last near the Tees, the earls disbanded their infantry and fled to Hexham. Here they were approached by the forces of Sir John Forster, the Lord Warden of the East March, coming across from Newcastle. On 19 December there was a skirmish with his scouts. This was the nearest approach to an engagement between the rebel and royal armies. From Hexham the earls, with a smaller body of horsemen, crossed the Pennines to Naworth, the Dacre stronghold. Sussex, Hunsdon and Sir Ralph Sadler reached Hexham, [complaining of 'extreme of frost and snow'] the day after they had left. Here they spent a bitterly cold Christmas; the earls were first reported to be protected by 'two notable thieves of Liddesdale', then they fled again across the Scottish border and sought haven among the clans that favoured Mary's cause. The chase was over and the pursuers turned their attention to the possibilities of gifts and rewards. Cecil was beset by 'cravers' for the Percy and Neville lands. Only the twenty-year-old Earl of Rutland, who had enthusiastically brought his tenants all the way from Belvoir, seems to have been sorry that the action had never begun. He wrote to Cecil for advice rather than estates: 'I am most willing to serve but all is at an end here.' Meanwhile Sussex noted the aptness of the 'occasion not only to settle all these parts in surety but to frame good government along the whole borders'. The long presidency of the Council of the North by the energetic puritan Earl of Huntington from 1572 to 1595 went some way towards doing this (**8**).

The rebellion had failed primarily because of its incoherence and aimlessness, but also because its support remained geographically limited. It had not even mobilised the full resources of the two earls, since Northumberland never had an opportunity to organise the raising of his own tenantry and only a mere eighty horsemen came to him on their own initiative. Across the Pennines several vital men failed to stir. Henry Clifford, the Earl of Cumberland, was a keen supporter of Mary but lacked vigour at the crucial moment. Leonard Dacre spent much of the autumn in London fighting a lawsuit against Norfolk over the duke's wardship of the Dacre children and his claim to their inheritance. When he returned to the north he fortified Naworth and gathered 3,000 men under the pretence of resisting the rebellion. But by January 1570 his loyalty was under suspicion and Elizabeth ordered his arrest. In February Hunsdon was attacked between Hexham and Carlisle by Dacre but defeated him in a pitched battle; 500 rebels were killed or captured but Dacre himself escaped to Scotland. If he had been at home earlier the response of Cumberland to the rising in November might have been much more energetic. As it was Lord Scrope, who had preserved order in Cumberland during the rising, excused his failure to bring troops to Sussex's assistance on 30 November by explaining that the county had 'for a few days stood in great peril'.

The rebellion was contained through the efforts of a small number of active men like Scrope, Sir Thomas Gargrave, the vice-president of the Council of the North, who held Pontefract and organised the mustering of royal troops in south Yorkshire, and Sir John Forster, who was hard pressed to maintain his hold on Northumberland and the Berwick area. Sussex did everything he could with the resources available to him and cannot be blamed for allowing the rebellion to last five weeks. On 26 November Hunsdon, commending him to Cecil, pointed out that 'yf hys dyllygence and carfulness had not been gret, her Majestye had neyther had Yorke nor Yorksher at thys ower att hyr devocyon and commandment'. Sadler held the same view [**doc. 23**].

The rebellion had been almost bloodless. Apart from the skirmish between Dacre and Hunsdon, the only loss of life had been in the siege of Barnard Castle when five men were killed and some more killed themselves leaping over the walls to desert. The rebels had contented themselves with destroying the barns, crops and cattle of those gentry who would not join them. The blood shed in the government's orgy of revenge was in marked contrast to the rebels' attitude to their victims. Elizabeth ordered that 700 of the rank and file should be executed by martial law. The evidence is too incomplete for it to be possible to reach a precise estimate of the number of executions actually carried out, but it is clear from the papers of Sir George Bowes, the provost marshal, that the Queen's intentions were not fulfilled (**68**). For Richmondshire and for eighteen townships of the Darlington ward of County Durham the list of those who were executed has survived as well as the list of those pricked by Sussex to suffer. These lists show that Bowes, who found the whole task distasteful, did not adhere to the letter of the Lord President's orders. He was prevented from doing so because, as he explained to Sussex, 'although I have both by day and night caused to search their towns they be wholly fled'. In Darlington ward only twenty-four of the forty-one appointed died. In Richmondshire the proportion was 57 out of 215.

Although there is less evidence about what happened in the rest of Yorkshire it would not be surprising if many escaped elsewhere, considering that Bowes, urged on by Sussex and the queen, had to carry out his circuit of the whole area affected by the rebellion in three weeks in terrible winter conditions. He complained of his difficulties to Sussex on 8 January: 'The circuit of my commission is great, the several places where the prisoners were taken far distant, the weather extreme and the country (except in the bottom ways) impassable for snow.'

48472

Sussex's letters to the Queen about the executions are certainly untrustworthy evidence because, in order to satisfy her drive for severity, he tended to report that they were complete for a particular area before Bowes could possibly have had time to carry out orders which Sussex had himself only just despatched. Bowes later wrote in his general memorandum on the rebellion that he did not know how many executions were carried out in Bywell lordship, Hexhamshire and Northumberland as Sir John Forster was responsible for these areas. But the number condemned in the marches was anyway small; even if Forster carried out his orders more thoroughly than Bowes the maximum number of those who suffered by martial law seems to be about 450.

A number of the rebel leaders escaped abroad. The Earl of Westmoreland, Richard Norton and three of his sons and Thomas Markenfeld reached the Netherlands where they lived as pensioners of Spain. Northumberland was less lucky. Betrayed by a border clan to the Scottish regent he was handed over to Lord Hunsdon at Berwick in June 1572. He made no attempt to evade the searching questions on his part in the rebellion that Hunsdon put to him [**doc. 24**]. He was beheaded at York in August 1572. Eight of the leaders captured immediately after the rebellion, including two of the Nortons, had suffered at Tyburn in 1570, but many of the gentry involved had been allowed to purchase their lives by handing over their lands and possessions to the Crown. Both Cecil and Sussex were most concerned in 1570 with recouping the expenses of the vast army that had marched north to no purpose. It was John Knox, writing to Cecil, who saw the real significance of the first two years of Mary's captivity in England: 'If you strike not at the root, the branches that appear to be broken will bud again with greater force.'

THE CAUSES OF THE REBELLION

The earls entered into rebellion because they were desperate men who felt they had been driven into a corner. Northumberland in his confession explained how they were persuaded that they must rebel or flee (**doc. 24**). At Brancepeth he resisted those who were 'earnest to proceed', until he saw he had no alternative but to join them. Francis Norton's account confirms that there was no definite plan until Norfolk's departure from court, when the north heard of 'the Queen's displeasure towards him and others of the nobility': 'We thought there would be some great stir, which caused us to confer together at divers times.' The earls did not take the initiative in these discussions. When it came to action they were in fact only leaders by virtue of their position as feudal superiors. Northumberland's timidity was commented on by Hunsdon, writing to Cecil, on 26 November: 'He ys very tymerus, and yt ys affyrmde, hathe ment, twyse or thryse, too sybmytt hymselfe, but that hys wyfe beyng the stower of the too, dothe hasten hym, and yncorage hym to persever'. Neither of the earls had the energy of their wives. The Countess of Northumberland rode with the army through Yorkshire and later proved herself an inveterate plotter with Don John of Austria on behalf of Mary Queen of Scots (**95,** p. 225)

Four men can be identified as the main agitators who instigated the rebellion: Richard Norton, the eighty-one-year-old sheriff of Yorkshire; Christopher Neville; Thomas Markenfeld, Norton's son in law; and Dr Morton. It was Christopher Neville, Westmoreland's uncle, who was largely responsible for securing the young earl's participation in the rising. Bowes emphasised Neville's influence over his nephew in his letters to Sussex. Christopher Neville's motives may have been genuinely religious, but he was of a violent nature anyway. In 1554 he had been involved in a riot with three northern families the Rokebys, the Bowes and the Wycliffes, at Gatherley Races. The feud was evidently still alive in 1569; while Neville was prominent among the rebels, the heads of all these three families were involved in the defence of Barnard Castle.

There is no doubt that the other three agitators acted from an enthusiastic belief in the Catholic cause. Markenfeld and Morton had gone to the continent earlier in Elizabeth's reign and returned in 1568 fired with the enthusiasm of the Counter reformation. Northumberland tells of an interview with Morton, during which he spoke of the need to awake the lethargic north and 'lamented the want of sound Catholic priests to whom he might give authority to reconcile such people as would seek it'. Francis Norton later said that Morton was 'the most earnest mover of the rebellion'; he drove them on by warning them of 'dangers touching our souls and the loss of our country'. Richard Norton, who had worn the badge of the Five Wounds of Christ in the Pilgrimage of Grace, certainly seems to have been influenced by Morton's arguments. Markenfeld answered those who doubted the legitimacy of rising before the promised Papal Bull had been published, by maintaining that 'the Queen was excommunicated when she refused to suffer the Pope to send his ambassador to her presence'.

Northumberland felt a deep and passionate concern for his faith **[doc. 24]**. Sir Thomas Gargrave reported in 1572 that 'at or before his dethe he contynewed obstynate in relygyon' and 'affermyd this realme was in a scysme'. He also had bitter personal grievances against the Queen. Northumberland had suffered severely from Elizabeth's reassertion of the policies of her father, aimed at weakening the hold of the great magnate families on the marches. She had deprived him of his Wardenship of the Middle March and allowed him no part in the custody of Mary. In 1568 the crown had ignored his claim for compensation over the rights to the copper mine discovered at Newlands on one of his estates. Northumberland had declined in wealth as well as status. In 1562 he had written to the Earl of Pembroke that he was forced to 'humblie request her highnes to disburs unto me a thousand pounds, or more, if it may be conveniently granted . . . otherwise in good faieth I knowe not what shift I shal be able to maik'. The Earl of Westmoreland was also suffering from poverty. In 1568 he had to borrow eighty pounds from Sir George Bowes. Yet despite all these grievances the Earls were most unwilling to rebel; Northumberland maintained in his confession that he 'was drawn into it per force'.

Many of the gentry involved in the rebellion were retainers of the earls. An analysis of the geography of gentry support for the rising shows that the largest groups came from Brancepeth and Topcliffe, the seats of the Nevilles and Percies, while several gentry came from Raby, the other seat of the Nevilles. The custom under which the sons of northern gentry families served in the households of the great magnates enabled the earls to attain the support of such men as John Sayer and Marmaduke Redman, servants to Northumberland. Redman's father remained neutral but Sayer's actively assisted Bowes in the defence of Barnard Castle. Both Sadler and Hunsdon comment on the way the rebellion split family loyalties (**doc. 23**). The Council of the North mentioned this to the Queen: 'Many gentlemen show themselfs ready to serve your Majestie, whose sons and heirs, or other sons, be on the other side.' It seems likely that heads of families were too cautious to risk losing their material possessions in the hope of a return to catholicism.

The strength of the rebel army lay in their horsemen, who were 'gentlemen and ther household servants and tenants'. Such men joined the earls through bastard feudal allegiance. Tenant loyalty goes some way towards explaining the participation of the commons as well. 'The Erle of Northumberland hathe the keepinge of Myddleham, and steward of Rychmond', wrote Lord Hunsdon to Cecil, 'whereby he hathe nowe a grete part of hys force too serve agaynst the Queen'. The lists of rebels pardoned show that Richmond and Middleham were among the towns which contributed the largest number of the commons. But the appeal to bastard feudal loyalty was insufficient in itself to raise a large army; the rebel leaders resorted to religious propaganda, the offer of wages and the threat of spoil in their recruitment drive. Sir John Forster wrote, on 24 November, that he had just heard that 'the Earls have offered wages of sixteen pence a day to all that will come'. Many undoubtedly joined the rebellion because they feared for their lives and goods. On 17 November Bowes reported to Cecil: 'They have constreined, by force, sundrie to followe them; as the people of Bishopton, tenants of John Conyers, my sonne-in-law . . . they not only forced them to go with them, but compelled the rest of the towne, armed, and unarmed, to go to Darneton.' He told Cecil two days later that 'the people compelled to go against their wills, are all ready to mutiny, and many stealethe away'.

The earls' proclamations consistently emphasised the religious issue [**doc. 22**]. The official ground of the rebellion was to resist the 'new found religion and heresie' imposed since Elizabeth came to the throne. The earls gave a nationalist as well as a catholic slant to their propaganda. Sussex wrote to Cecil on 17 November: 'They persuade that their cause of seeking to reform religion is that other princes have determined to do it, and this entering of strangers should be troublesome to the realm, and therefore they seek to do it before their coming'. The proclamations were part of a carefully planned campaign to attract the support of the commons. At the Durham demonstration Richard Norton led the rebels into the city carrying that emotive symbol of northern discontent, the banner of the Five Wounds of Christ. But Bowes's report of an incident at Darlington on 16 November reveals the hollowness of this campaign: 'Masse was yesterday at Darnton; and John Swinburn, with a staffe, drove before him the poor folks, to hasten them to hear the same' (**95,** p. 227).

The Earl of Sussex was convinced that the people flocked to the earls because they 'like so well their cause of religion'. But Sussex, unable to leave York, was not in a position to form an accurate impression of the motives of the commons. It was natural that a man like Sir Thomas Gargrave, vice-president of the Council of the North, should see the rising in religious terms. He was a convinced protestant, anxious about the future of his faith in the north. In his account of how the rebellion began he emphasised the failure of the religious settlement to take hold in the north: 'I would wish some strict laws, and especially for the exercise of the open service and sacrement, being refused by many, and likely thereby to be brought much into contempt.' Sir Ralph Sadler similarly wrote of the deep religious conservatism of the people, gentry and commons alike [**doc. 23**]. 'The ancient faith still lay like lees at the bottom of men's hearts and if the vessell was ever so little stirred came to the top'; this was how he thought the conspirators gained their support.

The Elizabethan religious settlement had made little impact in the north during the first decade of the reign. A recent study of the York Ecclesiastical Commission has shown that it was merely 'attempting to induce or maintain any form of conformity, however shallow' (**80,** p. 38). Cecil estimated in 1566 that two-thirds of the northern justices were catholic. In November 1568 the Earl of Sussex and his council reported that many churches had had no sermons for years past; it was difficult to get preachers to travel and the ignorance of the people was the main cause of their backwardness in religion. Professor Dickens concluded, from a study of the visitation books for the years 1567–8, that 'there existed no recusant problem in the diocese of York'; but he did find plenty of evidence of vague conservatism and popular uncertainty about giving up long practised rituals (**56**). There were cases of the use of holy water, images and candles; in the Vale of York some priests were prepared to defy the government by saying the communion for the dead.

The demonstration which was organised and maintained over several weeks at Durham, during the rebellion, shows how responsive the people could be to a revival of catholic ritual and practice. In this case a strong lead was given by a group of determined priests. They gained control of the cathedral services and mass was openly said to large congregations, which included canons, choristers, lay clerks, and many poorer citizens. William

Holmes, one of the leading spirits, claimed that he had authority to reconcile the people to the Church of Rome and pronounced absolution to the kneeling congregation. But it needed the enthusiasm of someone like Holmes to activate northern catholic emotion. Professor Dickens concluded from his investigation of early Yorkshire recusancy that the characteristic of northern catholicism was one of 'survivalism' (**56**). Until the Jesuits arrived the catholic tradition was one of 'withdrawal from the Elizabethan order in favour of something older' (**51**). No one had prepared the ground for Morton and Markenfeld. The catholicism they found in the north was merely habitual and uninformed: 'a set of ingrained observances which defined and gave meaning to the cycle of the week and the seasons of the year, to birth, marriage and death' (**51**). The earls found that religious propaganda alone was not enough because rebellion contradicted such a tradition. It was a tradition that led to inertia not activity, grudging obedience not resistance.

So it is the secular rather than religious tensions of northern society which now deserve serious consideration in the context of this rebellion. It may well be that political resentment at the extension of Tudor authority in the north was more important in attracting support to it than hatred of protestantism. Bowes was hated not for his religious feelings but for his notorious loyalty. Elizabeth had deliberately built up the gentry clientele of Northumberland's rival, Sir John Forster, and had put her cousin, Lord Hunsdon, in charge of Berwick and the East March. The rebellion has recently been interpreted as 'the last episode in 500 years of protest by the Highland Zone against the interference of London' (**38**, p. 251). When Elizabeth summoned the earls to court she precipitated a crisis in northern society: the cause of catholicism proved inadequate to sustain the rising that followed. The failure of the rebellion, its feebleness and its disorganisation, all proved that northern feudalism and particularism could no longer rival Tudor centralisation.

Part Three

ASSESSMENT

9 Rebellion and Tudor Government

The aura of Tudor monarchy and the theory of obligation the dynasty developed were so strong that Tudor rebels did not dare to challenge the crown directly. Only the Kentish rising of 1554 can be credited with a coherent plan to overthrow the monarch, and even then many of Wyatt's supporters saw the rising as a demonstration against the Spanish marriage rather than an attack on the Queen's authority. Rebels normally tried to avoid the accusation of treason by finding scapegoats among chief ministers. In 1536 it was Cromwell, in 1569 Burghley, who were to blame for the grievances of the north. But the Tudor publicists emphasised that it was no more lawful to resist the king's ministers than the king himself. 'Ye resist your king if ye resist his proceedings', Nicholas Udall pointed out to the western rebels in 1549. He told them that they should petition to have the mass allowed in Cornish and that in the matter of the gentry and their servants 'it is lawful for every man to put up his bill to the King's majesty's high court of parliament for anything that he thinketh expedient for a commonweale'. But parliament was effectively closed to the mass of the people and when men rebelled they were driven on by strongly emotional material or spiritual needs. Their articles represented their blunt attempt at petitioning. 'They stand for patient reformation and yet must they tarry a parliament time', wrote Somerset of the Norfolk rebels to Lord Russell in July 1549. This comment highlights the dilemma of the Tudor monarchy. Even if the king's servants saw that the demonstrators had a case, rebellion was treason and must be crushed.

Every Tudor monarch faced at least one major rebellion during his or her reign. If Stoke in 1487 was the last battle of the Wars of the Roses, Henry VII could not feel secure while Perkin Warbeck and Lambert Simnel prolonged the aftermath of the struggle of York and Lancaster. The resistance to the taxation demands of the first two Tudors taught them that their rule depended on the support of the taxpaying classes. In 1525 Henry VIII learnt that there were limits beyond which the taxpayers could not be pushed.

Eleven years later Henry VIII was faced by the first of the four major rebellions which were concentrated into eighteen years of the mid-century. The period 1534–58 was marked by radical religious policies and the inadequate Edwardian and Marian monarchies. Tudor society was under the increasing pressure of inflation and the economy did not expand to accommodate a growing population. A comprehensive analysis of the popular sedition and disorder of this period as a whole is needed. A recent thesis on the reign of Mary has suggested that the period 1553–8 was one of 'permanent crisis' (**76, 18**). If similar studies of the crises of the Henrician and Edwardian reformations, and perhaps the period 1568–72 also, become available, some interesting comparisons will be possible. Meanwhile many questions about the seriousness of the opposition these Tudor governments faced and the efficiency of their security systems must remain open. How competent, for instance, was Sir Francis Walsingham's spy system compared with Thomas Cromwell's? It is clear that the rebellions of these years raised worrying military problems. There is no evidence that the Duke of Norfolk had difficulty in obtaining recruits for an army against the Pilgrimage of Grace in 1536 but he was never happy about how they would behave if it came to armed conflict. The Pilgrimage was defeated by bluff. Protector Somerset had to rely to a great extent on foreign mercenaries to crush the disorders of 1549. The rebellions that summer made the gentry feel very insecure. Sir Thomas Wyatt may not have been the only gentleman who took his own initiative in planning or forming a local militia against future rioting [**doc. 20**] (**94,** pp. 163–80).

In 1549 Protector Somerset faced more determined and widespread popular opposition than any other Tudor government, caused by exasperation at his failure to combine good intentions to relieve want and poverty with effective action. The social idealists, like Robert Crowley and Hugh Latimer, spoke and wrote of the needs of the Commonwealth, as against the self interest of the 'gredye cormerauntes', the rentraisers, engrossers and forestallers: 'We have good statues made, as touching commoners and inclosers, many meetings and sessions, but in the end of the matter there cometh nothing forth' (**39,** p. 57). In this situation the harmony of Tudor society collapsed and class hostility flared up in several areas. 'All have conceived a wonderful hate against gentlemen and taketh them all as their enemies', wrote Somerset. Alexander Neville recounted that in Norfolk 'so hated at this time was the name of worship or gentleman that the basest of the people, burning with more than hostile hatred, desired to extinguish and utterly cut off the gentry'. Cranmer expressed his horror at the western rebels' attempt to limit the gentry's servants: 'Standeth it with any reason to turn upside down the good order of the whole world, that is everywhere and hath been, that is to say the commoners to be governed by the nobles and the servants by their masters?' In 1549 the gentry were scapegoats for those with religious, as much as those with economic, grievances. The rising at Seamer in Yorkshire against the Edwardian reformation consisted, according to Foxe, of a plan 'at first rushe to kill and destroy such gentlemen and men of substance about them, as were favourers of the kynges procedynges, or which would resiste them' (**55**). Foxe says that four gentry were taken and murdered: 'After they had strypped them of their clothes and purses, they left them naked behynd them in the playne fields for crowes to feede on' (**91,** pp. 452–3).

The disorders of Edward VI's reign did not end with the fall of Somerset. The Privy Council register refers to commotions in 1550 in the west, Nottinghamshire, Kent and elsewhere, which were serious enough for the men of the Boulogne garrison to be distributed in the disaffected counties. In September 1551 an intended insurrection in Leicestershire, Northamptonshire and Rutland, by 'certain light knaves, horsecoursers and craftsmen', was reported to Lord Admiral Clinton (**92,** pp. 56–69, 427–34).

The continuing insecurity of the Marian government has been fully investigated. (**76, 18**). When in the first year of her reign Mary found herself challenged by Sir Thomas Wyatt she was saved only by the loyalty of a section of the nobility and their retainers. From then on her government was frequently harassed by alarms. In 1555 the Privy Council thought it necessary to forbid the normal mid-summer festivities lest they should be used as an excuse for rioting. The government feared that internal disorder was inspired by agitation from abroad, so treated even minor rebellions such as that at Diss in Norfolk in 1556, with the utmost seriousness. This inefficient affair was an attempt by the local schoolmaster to proclaim Mary's death and the joint accession of Elizabeth and Courtenay. He read a proclamation at Yaxley church then 'seeine yt hys partye was so weake . . . beganne to flee'. D. M. Loades has concluded that the opposition in Mary's reign 'was able to sustain an erratic but unnerving pressure which could never be ignored or treated lightly' (**76**).

The mid-century period then made obvious the need for both more emphatic government propaganda against rebellion and the organisation of a proper militia system. William Cecil gave both these matters his close attention (**5, 9, 20**). The reigns of Edward VI and Mary had also seen the undoing of much of Henry VIII's achievement in substituting royal for magnate power in the north. Mary had restored the Earl of Northumberland to his estates. She had relied for defence of the north against the Scots in 1557 on the old established magnate families, the Earls of Shrewsbury, Northumberland, Westmoreland and Derby. Elizabeth reasserted her father's policies and drove the earls into rebellion. Professor Stone has emphasised that the 'decisive shift' from governing as medieval kings had done 'mainly with the cooperation of the aristocracy . . . to dependence on the squirearchy and gentry' only occurred in the later years of Elizabeth's reign (**38**, p. 256). The two great northern rebellions of 1536 and 1569 were important stages in this process.

The revolt of the Earl of Essex in 1600 forms a postscript to the story of the collapse of aristocratic rebellion. Essex and his followers at court rebelled as a desperate gamble. They were suffering from thwarted ambition and deteriorating finances (**38**, p. 481). The rebellion was no more than a foolish and aimless riot but if it had achieved any success in London it might have received considerable support from the Earl's Welsh tenantry (**38**, p. 255). In fact it finally proved the bankruptcy of armed rebellion as an instrument of court politics.

'There is nothing will sooner lead men into sedition', Lord Burghley said, 'than dearth of victual.' Although the years 1595–8 saw no major rebellion it can be argued that this was one of the most insecure periods of Tudor government. The panic legislation of the 1597–8 parliament reflected this insecurity (**25**, vol. 2, p. 335). There was a crisis of subsistence: a dramatic inflation of prices and a disastrous drop in wages led to starvation and weakened resistance to infection (**17**). Professor Hoskins has described the graph of the fluctuations in the average price of wheat from year to year as 'the heartbeats of the whole economy of England' (**62**). In these years, when the heartbeats were very slow, men rioted through sheer hunger.

In 1596 there was a rising in Oxfordshire based on the villages of Hampton Gay and Hampton Poyle, which had been much enclosed by local gentry. The plan, until the ringleaders were arrested by the Lord Lieutenant, was to seize arms and horses from the houses of the gentry and join the London apprentices who were rumoured to have rebelled. In Norfolk in 1597 the commons assembled near Lynn and forcibly unloaded a barge laden with corn bound for Gainsborough. At Canterbury the same year the commons of the poor suburb of St Dunstans, unable to obtain food, stopped two carts carrying corn on Watling Street, after hearing rumours that it was being exported to France. Much grain was in fact exported from Faversham at this time and Kent also supplied a large proportion of the London market. In 1596 the Privy Council had overruled an attempt by the Lord Lieutenant of the county to prohibit grain shipment from Kent to London.

What then were the patterns and themes of the rebellions of the sixteenth century? They have the character of demonstrations. They were pursued with varying degrees of order and organisation according to the capability of the gentry leadership and the emotional force of the issues involved. On the whole Tudor rebellions were remarkably non-violent. The outbursts of violence and victimisation, the murder of Body or the Bishop of Lincoln's chancellor for instance, were isolated incidents that stand out from what were essentially movements of peaceful resistance to specific government policies (**89**).

Only one clear theme of national significance ran through the rebellions. This was the opposition of a conservative and pious society to the English Reformation. The symbol of reaction was the banner of the Five Wounds, which was carried in 1536, 1549 and again in 1569: the Church was in danger, rituals and customs which were known and treasured because they had become habitual were being abolished. The growth of English protestantism was a long and tortuous process and little was done in the Tudor period to teach the new faith in the counties furthest from London. The religious motives of Tudor rebels were motives of uncertainty and bewildered insecurity. The rebels were parochial because local chantries, shrines and monasteries were of more significance to them than new statements of faith from London. In most cases they tried to beseige the provincial capital, for example Exeter, Carlisle or Norwich. And their agrarian grievances took their distinctive form from the character of particular farming regions (**41**) [**docs. 9, 17**].

Tudor Rebellions then were essentially the responses of local communities to local grievances. The main thing they had in common was their provincialism. The Levellers took up this provincial thinking in the 1640s. Their third Agreement of the People called for the abolition of the law courts in London and the substitution of regional courts administered by locally elected sheriffs and J.P.s. An examination of the programme of the Levellers, in the light of late medieval and Tudor rebellions, reveals that there was also a persistent egalitarian tradition from 1381 to 1649 (**87**). The ideas of John Wycliffe and John Ball were submerged for much of the Tudor period because social equality was identified with anabaptism and was thus hated and feared. Egalitarianism emerged occasionally though with startling and dramatic force. The tensions of 1549 brought it to the surface. It formed a strong element in the prophecies which circulated the country and which a superstitious age took so seriously. Foxe quotes as a cause of the Seamer rising 'the blind and phantasticall prophecie' that king, nobles and gentry would be swept away in favour of four governors supported by a parliament of the commons (**55; 100,** pp. 463–4). Kett's mention of the Grand Manumission of Calvary is a faint echo of the much more violent egalitarianism that pervaded the German peasant risings. It was the belief in equality based on the Christian view of the brotherhood of man that caused Rainborough to make his famous claim at the Putney debates in 1647 on behalf of the freedom and rights of the poorer members of society (**37**).

Part Four

DOCUMENTS

THE DUKE OF NORFOLK TO WOLSEY 1525

The Duke of Norfolk made this report from Lavenham on 11 May 1525. The gathering of the Suffolk commons was the nearest approach by those who resisted the Amicable Grant to open rebellion.

Pleas it your grace to bee advertised that this day at x a clock we the Duke of Norfolk and Suffolk met to gethers at a place appoyntid ii myles on this syde Bury with all the company of bothe the shires which was a right goodly company to loke upon at the leste iiii thousand whiche were gatherd sithnis Tuisday in the mornyng. And unto us cam the inhabitants of the towne of Lavenham and brant Ely whiche were offenders to a great nombre. They cam all in theire shirtts and kneling before us with pitious crying for pity shewed that they were the kings moste humble and faithefull subgiatts and so wold contynu during theire lyves saying that this offence by them comitted was only for lack of worke so that they knewe not howe to gett theire lyvinge. And for theire offence moste humbly besought us to bee meanes to the kings highnes for pardon remission, unto whome we made a long rehersall the beste we could to agravate theire haynous offence declaring the same to bee highe treason and laying the soreste we could to theire charge as well of theire evell demeanour againste the kings highnes as of theire rayling words. Finally we [chose] out iiii of the pryncipall of the offenders . . . we gave all the reste leave to departe save those iiii with as sharp and sore lessons any more to do like offence as we could devyce.

B.M. Cotton MSS, Cleopatra F.VI. 325; *Letters and Papers of Henry VIII*, iv (1) 1323.

THE EXAMINATION OF NICHOLAS LECHE 1536

Nicholas Leche, the priest of Belchford, took the initiative in raising the commons around Horncastle. He was tried for treason and executed at Tyburn in March 1537. His examination throws interesting light on the cooperation of the gentry and commons in Lincolnshire but it should be treated with caution since it is likely that Leche did his utmost to dissociate himself from the leadership of the rising.

The gentlemen were always together commonly a mile from the commons. What they did he knows not, but at length they brought forth certain articles of their griefs, of which one was that the King should remit the subsidy, and another he should let the abbeys stand, which articles George Stanes openly proclaimed in the field, and the sheriff and he, about Langwith field, said to the commons, 'Masters ye see that in all the time we have been absent from you we have not been idle. How like you these articles? If they please you say Yea. If not, ye shall have them amended.' The commons then held up their hands and said with a loud voice, 'We like them very well'.

Amongst other articles there declared, Mr Sheriff and other gentlemen said, 'Masters, there is a statute made whereby all persons be restrained to make their wills upon their lands, for now the eldest son must have all his father's lands, and no person to the payment of his debt, neither to the advancement of his daughter's marriages, can do nothing with their lands, nor cannot give his youngest son any lands'. Before this he thinks that the commons knew not what the Act of Uses meant. Nevertheless, when that article was read to them, they agreed to it as to all other articles devised by the gentlemen. He thinks all the exterior acts of the gentlemen amongst the commons were done willingly, for he saw them as diligent to set forward every matter as the commons were. And further, during the whole time of the insurrection, not one of them persuaded the people to desist or showed them it was high treason. Otherwise he believes in his conscience they would not have gone forward, for all the people with whom he had intelligence thought they had not offended the King, as the gentlemen caused proclamations to be made in his name. He thinks the gentlemen might have stayed the people of Horncastle, for at the beginning his parishioners went forward among the rebels only by command of the gentlemen. The gentlemen were first harnessed of all others, and commanded the commons to prepare themselves harness, and he believes the commons expected to have redress of grievances by way of supplication to the King.

Letters and Papers of Henry VIII, xii (1), 70 (xi) (**81,** pp. 210–11; **89,** pp. 21, 24–5).

document 3

THE YORK ARTICLES 1536

These are the articles which Robert Aske wrote out and sent to the Mayor of York when he yielded to the pilgrims' summons on 15 October.

To the Kyng our Soveraign lorde.

1. The suppression of so many religiouse howses as are at this instant tyme suppressed, whereby the service of our God is not wel [maintained] but also the [commons] of yor realme be unrelevyd, the which as we think is a gret hurt to the common welthe and many sisters be [put] from theyr levyings and left at large.

2. The second article is that we humbly beseache your grace that the acte of use may be suppressed because we think by the sayd act we your true subiects be clearly restrayned of yor liberties in the declaration of our wylles concernying our landes, as well for payment of our dettes, for doeing of yor grace service, as for helping and alevying of our children, the which we had by the . . . of yor lawes by . . . the which as we think is a gret hurt and . . . to the commonwelth.

3. The iiiide article is that weyr your grace hath a taxe or a quindeyne granted unto you by act of parliament payable the next year, the which is and hath been ever leveable of shepe and catals, and the shepe and catals of yor subjects within the sayde shire are now at this instant tyme in manner utterly decayed and . . . whereby your grace to take the sayde tax or quindeyn yor sayde subjects shalbe distrayned to paye iiiid for every beast and xiid for xxtie shepe, the which wold be an importunate charge to them considering the poverty that they be in all redye and losse which they have sutayned these ii years by past.

4. The iiiith article is that we wor yor true subjects thinke that yor grace takes of yor counsell and being a boute you such persons as be of low byrth and small reputation which hath procuryed the proffits most especially for theyr own advantage, the which we suspect to be the lord cromwell and Sir Richard Riche Chanceler of the augmentations.

5. The vth article is that we your true subjects fynd us grevyd that there be diverse bisshopes of England of yor Graces late promosion that hath ... the faith of Christ, as we thinke, which are the bisshops of Canterbury, the bisshop of Rochester, the bisshop of Worcester, the bisshop of Salisbury, the bisshop of Saint Davids, and the bisshop of Dublyn, and in especiall we thynk the begynyngs of all the trouble of that ... and the vexation that hath been ... of yor subjects the bisshop of Lincoln.

Letters and Papers of Henry VIII, xi, 705 (1).

document 4

THE OATH OF THE HONOURABLE MEN 1536

Robert Aske later explained that he 'made and devised the Oath . . . without any other man's advice' before the council of the pilgrim captains held at York on 17 October. Here it was administered to the gentlemen and it was then taken by all the pilgrims.

Ye shall not enter into this our Pilgrimage of Grace for the Commonwealth, but only for the love that ye do bear unto Almighty God his faith, and to Holy Church militant and the maintainance thereof, to the preservation of the King's person and his issue, to the purifying of the nobility, and to expulse all villein blood and evil councillors against the commonwealth from his Grace and his Privvy Council of the same. And that ye shall not enter into our said Pilgrimage for no particular profit to yourself, nor to do any displeasure to any private person, but by counsel of the commonwealth, nor slay nor murder for no envy, but in your hearts put away fear and dread, and take afore you the Cross of Christ, and in your hearts His faith, the Restitution of the Church, the suppression of these Heretics and their opinions, by all the holy contents of this book.

Letters and Papers of Henry VIII, xi, 705 (4) (**99,** p. 209).

ROBERT ASKE TO THE LORDS AT PONTEFRACT 1536

Robert Aske wrote this account of his interview with the lords and gentry at Pontefract on 19 October when he was in London in December 1536. It was written at Henry's request.

And to the lords temporal, the said Aske declared they had misused themselves, in that they, semblable, had not so providently ordered and declared to his said highness the poverty of his realm, and that part specially, and wherein their griefs might ensue, whereby all dangers might have been avoided; for insomuch as in the north parts much of the relief of the commons was by succour of abbeys, and that before this last statute thereof made, the King's highness had no money out of that shire in a manner yearly, for his grace's revenues there yearly went to the finding of Berwick. And that now the profits of abbeys suppressed, tenths and first fruits, went out of those parts. By occasion whereof, within short space or years, there should be no money nor treasure in those parts, neither the tenant to have to pay his rents to the lord, nor the lord to have money to do the King service withal, for so much as in those parts was neither the presence of his grace, execution of his laws, nor yet but little recourse of merchandise, so that of necessity the said country should either patyssh with the Scots, or of very poverty enforced to make commotion or rebellions; and that the lords knew the same to be true and had not done their duty, for that they had not declared the said poverty of the said country to the King's highness, and the danger that otherwise his grace would ensue, alleging the whole blame to them the nobility therein with other like reasons.

Letters and Papers of Henry VIII, xii (1) 6; (**49**, p. 335 and **13**, p. 186).

document 6

THE PILGRIMS' BALLAD 1536

The pilgrims' ballad is thought to have been composed by the monks of Sawley Abbey in Lancashire. It has sixteen verses in all. This is only one of a number of rhymes circulated during the rising which combined the themes of the church in danger and the material needs of the commons.

I   Crist crucifyd!
For they woundes wide
Us commens guyde!
Which pilgrames be,
Thrughe godes grace,
For to purchache
Olde welth and peax
Of the spiritualtie

II   Gret godes fame
Doith Church proclame
Now to be lame
And fast in boundes,
Robbyd, spoled and shorne
From catell and corne,
And clene furth borne
Of housez and landes.

X   Alacke! Alacke!
For the church sake
Pore comons wake,
And no marvell!
For clere it is
The decay of this
How the pore shall mys
No tong can tell.

XI   For ther they hadde
Boith ale and breyde
At tyme of nede,
And succer grete
In alle distresse
And hevyness
And wel intrete

XII   In troubil and care,
Where that we were
In maner all bere
Of our substance,
We found good bate
At churche men gate,
Without checkmate
Or varyaunce.

XVI   Crim, crame, and riche
With thre ell and the liche
As sum men teache
God theym amend!
And that Aske may,
Without delay,
Here make a stay
And well to end.

Letters and Papers of Henry VIII, xi, 786 (3); (**49,** p. 344–5).

THE COMMONS OF WESTMORLAND TO LORD DARCY 1536

This letter of the pilgrim captains in Westmorland to ask Lord Darcy's advice is the only evidence of their demands.

... Consernynge the gyrsums for power men to be a laid a parte but only penny for penny gyrsum, with all the tythes to remayne to every man hys owne, doynge therfor accordynge to their dewtye, also taxes casten emongst the benefest men, as well them in abbett with in us as thai that is not incumbent for the commenwelthe. Which we dyssyre of your lordship to tendre up your plesur thairin watt we may do in all these causes for we thinke in our oppynon ytt we may putt in yair rowmes to serve God oder yt wald be glad to keep hospytallyte for sum of yam are no preestes yt hath ye benefyce in hand and oder of yam is my lord Cromwell chapplaynes ... we accept no getyllman of our counsel because we be affrayed of thaym. ...

Letters and Papers of Henry VIII, xi, 1080.

document 8

ADVICE TO THE PILGRIMS AT PONTEFRACT

This anonymous petition of advice to the pilgrims assembled at Pontefract has been convincingly attributed to Sir Thomas Tempest, who was ill and unable to attend in person. He had sat in the parliament of 1529–36 as member for Newcastle-on-Tyne. Aske seems to have been influenced by it at several points in drawing up the final articles.

My powre advyce to my lorde captayne, baronage and comynaltie at Pomf[rete] undyr ynsurreccyon that may be resuvyd with sysche of the Kyng's counsell as cummythe to Duncaster, where by me semys the Kyng schuld [condescend to] owr petecyon agaynst the Lowler and [trai]tur Thomas Crumwell, hys dyscypyles and adherentes or at leste exyle hym and theym furthe of the relm.

Firste, where yt ys a legyd that we schulde not tayke upon us to assyne his Gr[ace's Council] yt ys necessary that vertuus men that luffythe the communwelthe schulde be of his [counci]l . . . susche vertus men as woylde regarde the communwelthe abuffe their princys . . . in this nobyll reym who reydes the crownakylls of Edwarde the ii what juperdy he was in for Peres de G[ave]stun, Spenseres, and susche lyke cunsellars and . . . Rycharde the ii was deposyd for folowing the cunsell of susche lyke. Item, a prynce schulde be mayde Kynge to defende the realme, and rewle hys subietes vertuus[ly] be iutece myxyd with mercy and pyty, and not undur dysplesur by rygore to [p]u[t] men to de[the], for thowghe yt ys soyde that our bodes [be] the Kynges when he hayse kyllyd a man he [cannot] mayk a man a lyffe ayene.

Item, where yt ys alegyd that the Kynge hayfhe [au] toryte grantyd hym by parlamente to suppres theys abbays, I thynke that theys parlamentes was of nune actoryte nor vertu, for yff theys schulde be trewly namyd, they shulde be callyd counsylles of the Kynges [a]poyntment, and not parlaments, for parlamentes owyt to have the knyghtes of schyar and bur[gerses for the [t]owyns [at] ther owyne electyon that colde resun for the wellthe of the schyar or towyn . . . a parlament they have devysyd that men may not speke off the Kynges vycys whysch men may say trewly had moste nede to be spokyn on, and reformyd off [all] thyng, [for if] the the hẻde ayke how can the body be hole . . . but what so ever Crumwell says ys ryght and noyne but that.

Item, the false flatterer says he will make the King the richest prince in Christendom, but a man can have no more of us than we have, which in manner he has already, and yet not satisfied. I think he goes about to make him the poorest prince in Christendom, for when by such pillage he has lost the hearts of his baronage and poor commons, the riches of the realm are spent and his oath and faith broken, who will then love or trust him?

. . . hys servandes and ek hys servandes servandes thynkes to have the law in every playse here oyrderyd at their commandment, and wyll tayk upon thayme to commande scheryffe, justyays of peyse, coram, and of secyon in their mayster's name at their plesure, wytnes Brabsun and Dakynes, so that what so ever thay wyll have doyne must be lawfull, and who contrarys thaym shall be accusyd off tresun, be he never so trew a man.

Letters and Papers of Henry VIII, xi, 1244.

THE PONTEFRACT ARTICLES 1536

The document is headed 'Copie of the articles to the Lordes of the King's Cownsell at our comyng to Pontefract'. It can therefore be dated to 2–4 December.

1. The fyrst touchyng our faith to have the herezynes of Luther, Wyclif, Husse, Malanton, Ellecumpadus, Bucerus, Confessio Gemaniae, Apologia Malanctionis, the Works of Tyndall, of Barnys, of Marshall, of Rastall, Seynt Germayne and such other heresies of Anibaptist thereby within this realm be to annulled and destroyed.

2. The iid to have the supreme head of the church touching cure animarum to restored unto the see of Rome as before it was accustomyd to be, and to have the consecracions of the bysshops from hym without any first frutes or pencion to hym to be payd out of this realme or else a pension reasonable for the outward defence of our faith.

3. Item we humbly beseche our most dred sovereign lorde that the Lady Mary may be made legitimate and the former statute therein annulled, for the danger of the title that myght incurre to the crown of Scotland, that to be by parliament.

4. Item to have the abboyes suppressed to be restoryd unto theyr howses land and goodes.

5. Item to have the tenth and fyrst frutes clerely discharged of the same, onles the clergy wyll of themselvys graunte a rent charge in generality to the augmentacion of the crown.

6. Item to have the Freres Observauntes restorid unto ther houses agayn.

7. Item to have the heretiques, bisshoppes and temporall, and their secte to have condigne punyshment by fyer or such other, or ells to trye their quarell with us and our partie takers in batell.

8. Item to have the lord Cromwell, the Lord Chancellor, and Sir Richard Riche kniyght to have condyne punyshment, as the subverters of the good laws of this realem and maynteners of the false sect of those heretiques and the first inventors and bryngands in of them.

9. Item that the landes in Westmorland, Cumberland, Kendall, Dent, Sedber, Fornes and the abbayes landes in Mashamshire, Kyrkbyshire, Notherdale may be by tenant right, and the lord to have at every change ii years rent for gressom and no more according to the grante now made by the lordes to the comons there under ther seall. And this to be done by act of parliament.

10. Item the statutes of handgunnys and crossbowes to be repelled, and the . . . thereof onles it be in the Kings Forest or parkes for the kylling of his graces deer red and fallow.

11. Item that doctor Ligh and doctor Layton . . . have condigne punyshment for theyr extortions in theyr tyme of visitactions, as in [taking?] from religiouse howses xl li, xx li, and so to . . . summys, horses, . . . leases, under . . . brybes by them taken, and of theyr abhominable actes by them comytted and done.

12. Item reformation for the election of knights of shire and burgesses, and for the uses amonge the lordes in the parliament howse after theyr auncient custome.

13. Item statute for inclosors and intacks to put in execution, and that all intaks inclosors sith Ao iiii h vii to be pulled down except mountains, forest and parkes.

14. Item to be discharged of the quindene and taxes now granted by acte of parliament.

15. Item to have the parliament in a convenient place at Nottyngham or York and the same shortly somonyd.

16. Item the statute of the declaracion of the crown by wyll, that the same may be annulled and repellyd.

17. Item that it be inactid by acte of parliamente that all recognisances, statutues, penalties new forfayt during the tyme of this comocion may be pardonyd and discharged as well agaynst the King as strangers.

18. Item the privlages and rights of the church to be confirmed by acte of parliament, and prestes not suffre by sourde onless he be disgrecid, a man to be savid by his book, sanctuary to save a man for all causes in extreme nede, and the church for xl daies and further according to the laws as they were used in the begynnyng of this kings days.

19. Item the liberties of the church to have ther old custemys as the county palatyn at Durham, Beverlay, Ruppon, Sanct Peter of York and such other by act of parliament.

20. Item to have the statute that no man shall wyll hys lands to be repellid.

21. Item that the statutes of tresons for wordes and such lyke made since Ao xxi of our sovereign lord that now is to be in like wyse repelled.

22. Item that the comon lawes mai have place as was used in the begynning of your graces reyne and that all iniunctions may be clerely vewyed and not to be granted onles the mater be hard and determyned in the chancery.

23. Item that no man upon subpoena is from Trent north apeyr but at York or by attornay onles it be directid uppon payn of allegeance and for lyke maters concernyng the kyng.

24. Item a remedy ageynst eschaetors for fyndyng of fals offices and extorsions fees, taking which be not holdyn of the kyng and ageynst the . . . thereof.

Letters and Papers of Henry VIII, xi, 1246.

RICHARD MORRISON: A REMEDY FOR SEDITION 1536

In 1536 Richard Morrison returned to England after living in the household of Reginald Pole at Padua. His passage home was paid by Thomas Cromwell and he at once became one of the leading Cromwellian publicists (48, 85, chapter 4). His book A remedy for sedition was printed by Berthelet, the King's printer, within a few weeks of the outbreak of the Pilgrimage of Grace.

Whan every man wyll rule, who shall obeye? Nowe can there be any commune welthe, where he that is welthiest, is mooste lyke to come to woo? Who can there be ryche, where he that is rychest is in mooste daunger of povertie? No, no, take welthe by the hande, and say farewell welth, where lust is lyked, and lawe refused, where uppe is sette downe, and downe sette uppe: An order, an order muste be hadde, and a waye founde that they rule that beste can, they be ruled, that mooste it becommeth so to be. This agreement is not onley expedient, but also most necessary in a commonwelthe, those that are of the worser sort, to be content, that they wyser rule and governe theym, those that nature hath endued with syngular vertues, and fortune without breache of lawe, sette in high dignitie, to suppose this done by the great provydence of god, as a meane to engender love and amitie, betwene the high and the lowe, the smalle and the great, the one beinge so necessarye for the others savegarde welthe and quietnes. For as there must be some men of polycie and prudence, to discerne what is metest to be done in the government of states, even so there must be other of strength and redynes, to do what the wyser shall thinke expedient, bothe for the mayntenance of them that governe, and for the schuyng of the infinite jeoperdies, that a multitude not governed fallith into: These must not go, arme in arme, but the one before, the other behynde . . .

A comune welthe is lyke a body, and soo lyke, that it can be resembled to nothyng so convenient, as unto that. Nowe, were it not by your faythe, a madde herynge, if the fote shuld say, I wyl weare a cappe with an ouche, as the heade dothe? If the knees shulde say, we woll carie the eyes, an other wyle: if the shulders shulde clayme eche of them an eare: if the heles wold nowe go before, and the toes behind? This were undoubted a mad heryng: every man wold say, the fete, the knees, the shoulders, the heles make unlaufull requestes, and very madde petitions. But if it were so in dede, if the fote had a cap, the knees eies, the shulders eares, what a monstrous body shulde this be? God sende them suche a one, that shal at any time go about to make as evil a comune welth, as this is a body. It is not mete, every man to do, that he thinketh best.

THE EXAMINATION OF ROBERT ASKE 1537

Aske was examined about every aspect of his part in the Pilgrimage during his imprisonment in the Tower in April and May 1537. Both the interrogatories and his replies have been preserved.

To the statut of subpressions, he dyd gruge ayenst the same and so did al the holl contrey, because the abbeys in the north partes gaf great almons to pour men and laudable servyd God; in which partes of lait dais they had but smal comforth by gostly teching. And by occasion of the said suppression the devyn service of almightie God is much minished, greate nombre of messes unsaid, and the blissed consecracion of the sacrement now not used and showed in thos places, to the distreas of the faith, and spirituall comfort to man soull, the temple of God russed and pulled down, the ornamentes and releques of the church of God unreverent used, the townes and sepuleres of honourable and noble men pulled down and sold, non hospitalite now in thos places kept, but the fermers for the most parte lettes and taverns out the fermes of the same houses to other fermers, for lucre and advauntage to them selfes. And the profites of thies abbeys yerley goith out of the contrey to the Kinges highnes, so that in short space little money, by occasion of the said yerly rentes, tentes and furst frutes, should be left in the said countrey, in consideracion of the absens of the Kinges highnes in thos partes, want of his lawes and the frequentacion of merchandisse. Also diverse and many of the said abbeys wer in the montaignes and desert places, wher the people be rud of condyccions and not well taught the law of God, and when the said abbeys stud, the said peuple not only had worldly refreshing in their bodies but also spirituall refuge both by gostly liffing of them and also by spiritual informacion, and preching; and many ther tenauntes wer ther feed servaundes to them, and serving men, wel socored by abbeys; and now not only theis tenauntes and servauntes wantes refresshing ther, both of meat, cloth and wages, and knowith not now wher to have any liffing, but also strangers and baggers of come as betwix Yorkshir, Lancashir, Kendall,

Westmoreland and the bishopreke, was nither cariage of corne and merchandise, greatly socored both horsse and man by the said abbeys, for non was in thes partes denyed, nether horsemeat nor manesmeat, so that the people was greatlie refresshyed by the said abbeys, wher now they have no such succour; and wherfor the said statut of subpression was greatly to the decay of the comyn welth of that contrei and al thos partes of al degreys greatly groged ayenst the same, and yet doth ther dewtie of allegieance alwais savyd.

Also the abbeys was on of the bewties of this realme to al men and strangers passing threw the same; also al gentilmen much socored in their nedes with money, their yong sons ther socored, and in nonries ther doughters brought up in vertuee; and also ther evidenses and mony left to the usses of infantes in abbeys handes, alwas sure ther; and such abbeys as wer ner the danger of see bankes, great mayntenours of see wals and dykes, mayntenours and bilders of briges and heghwais, such other thinges for the comyn welth.

Letters and Papers of Henry VIII, xii (1) 852, 900, 901, 945, 946, 1175. Numbers 900, 901 and 945 are printed in full in the *English Historical Review*, v, 1890, 550–73.

THE DEMANDS OF THE WESTERN REBELS 1549

There are a number of different versions of the rebel articles. That printed here from A Copy of a Letter [**doc. 13**] *is the most complete and represents the final manifesto drawn up outside Exeter.*

The Articles of us the Commoners of Ddevonshire and Cornwall in divers Campes by East and West of Excettor.

1. Fyrst we wyll have the general counsall and holy decrees of our forefathers observed, kept and performed, and who so ever shal agayne saye them, we hold them as Heretikes.
2. Item we will have the Lawes of our Soverayne Lord Kyng Henry the viii concernynge the syxe articles, to be in use again, as in hys time they were.
3. Item we will have the masse in Latten, as was before, and celebrated by the Pryest wythoute any man or woman communycatyng wyth hym.
4. Item we wyll have the Sacrement hange over the hyeyhe aulter, and there to be worshypped as it was wount to be, and they whiche will not therto consent, we wyl have them dye lyke heretykes against the holy Catholyque fayth.
5. Item we wyll have the Sacramet of the aulter but at Easter delyvered to the lay people, and then but in one kynde.
6. Item we wil that our Curattes shal minister the Sacramet of Baptisme at all tymes aswel in the weke daye as on the holy daye.
7. Item we wyl have holy bread and holy water made every sondaye, Palmes and asshes at the tymes accustomed, Images to be set up again in every church, and all other auncient olde Ceremonyes used heretofore, by our mother the holy Church.
8. Item we wil not receyve the newe servye because it is but lyke a Christmas game, but we wyll have oure olde service of Mattens, masse, Evensong and procession in Latten not in English, as it was before. And so we the Cornyshe men (whereof certen of us understande no Englysh) utterly refuse thys newe Englysh.
9. Item we wyll have everye preacher in his sermon, and every Pryest at hys masse, praye specially by name for the soules in purgatory, as oure forefathers dyd.

10. Item we wyll have the whole Byble and al bokes of scripture in Englysh to be called in agayn, for we be enformed that otherwise the Clergye, shal not of log time confound the heretykes.

11. Item we wyll have Doctor Moreman and Doctor Crispin which holde our opinions to be savely sent unto us and to them we requyre the Kinges maiesty, to geve some certain lyvinges, to preach amonges us our Catholycke fayth.

12. Item we thinke it very mete because the lord Cardinal Pole is of the kynges bloode, should not only have hys free pardon, but also sent for to Rome and promoted to be first or secod of the kinges cousayl.

13. Item we wyll that no Gentylman shall have anye mo servantes then one to wayte upo hym excepte he maye dispende one hundreth marke land and for every hundreth marke we thynke it reasonable, he should have a man and no mo.

14. Item we wyll that the halfe parte of the abbey landes and Chauntrye landes, in everye mans possessyons, how so ever he cam by them, be geven again to two places, where two of the chief Abbeis was with in every Countye, where suche half part shalbe taken out, and there to be establyshed a place for devout persons, whych shall pray for the Kyng and the common wealth, and to the same we wyll have al the almes of the Churche box geven for these seven yeres, and for thys article we desire that we may name half of the Commissioners.

15. Item for the particular grieffes of our Countrye, we wyll have them so ordered, as Hunfreye Arundell, and Henry Braye the Kynges Maior of Bodma, shall enforme the Kynges Maiestye, yf they maye have salve-coduct under the Kynges great Seale, to passe and repasse, with an Heroalde of Armes.

16. Item for the performance of these articles we will have iiii Lordes viii Knightes xii Esquyers xx Yome, pledges with us untill the Kynges Maiestie have grounted al these by Parliament.

The articles are signed by the five 'chiefe captaynes' and 'the foure Governours of the Campes'.

Transcript from Lambeth Palace Library copy with the addition of the sixteenth article from the copy in Corpus Christi College, Oxford (**34,** App. K).

A COPY OF A LETTER 1549

Extract from A copy of a Letter, *printed tract of 1549. The letter was written by a gentleman of Devon on 27 July and gives a firsthand account of the rebellion and an analysis of its causes. There is some evidence to suggest that the recipient at court, Mr C. can be identified as Secretary Cecil. The letter comments on the price rise, the attitudes of gentry to their livings and the rebels' article on abbey and chantry lands.*

And if the comon people shalbe eased of their griefes, the gentel-men shall be relieved of them, for se how much the fermour crieth out of the market, the one as muche greved as the other, and one remedye I trust shal serve both. For me thinketh it is no more difference for me, to have xx pound, spedyng xx pound, than to have xx marke spendinge xx marke so that my estate be kept like with both, you wyll thynke I wryte now at my wyl, because yf ye remeber the last yere in the parke at Wynsour when the Court was there, thys question made great argument betwyxte you and me, whether for the amendment of thinges in the common wealthe the fermour should fyrst abate hys pryce, and then the Landed man his rent, or in contrary order, at whyche tyme, I remembre you stode upon one poynte, which I could not denye, that the Gentylman by deere byeng, was dryven to let deere, and I upon the other poynte (not al untrewe) that the deere hyrynge made a deere sellynge. But where the fault fyrst beganne, neyther of us woulde graunt to the other, neverthelesse, so wayghty a matter it is, as no wayes to be discussed but by Parliament. Where when the argument is at an ende, it may be establyshed by a lawe, wherof there was never more lykelyhood, because the amendment thereof, wyl helpe so many as well Lordes and Gentilme, as al other Commoners, no man havyng cause to repyne agaynst it, but suche as gather, not to spende and improve their lyvinges not for their charges, as many Gentilmen have done, but for their coffers. So that to conclude improvemet alone maketh no man ryche, but improvement and sparynge. But what medle I wyth thys matter, and yet what dare I not to you my fryende, by

137

Sayncte George I saye to you merely out of bourde, no one thinge maketh me more angry with these rebelles than one article, which toucheth me on the quicke, and I believe, there be few in the realme but it will make them smart, to forgoe his Abbey and Chauntrye landes wherein I for my part am so heated, that if I should fight wyth those traitours, I wold for every two strokes to be stricken for treason strike on to kepe my lands, the which I bought to suerlye, to deliver it at a papistes appoyntement.

Transcript from Lambeth Palace Library copy (**34,** App. K).

NICHOLAS UDALL'S ANSWER TO THE COMMONERS OF DEVONSHIRE AND CORNWALL 1549

Nicholas Udall (1505–56), a protestant convert while at Oxford, became Headmaster of Eton but was dismissed in 1541 after being involved in certain scandals. He later gained the favour of Edward VI through the patronage of Catherine Parr (22). This extract from his Answer to the commons in 1549 *illustrates two themes in his writing: the vividness with which he depicted the results of rebellion and his strident confidence in the protestant cause.*

What other fruit or end may hereof ensue unto you but devouring one another and an universal desolation of your own selves, besides the extreme peril of God's high wrath and indignation, besides the undoubted plague of mortality which (unless ye call for mercy in season) must needs light upon you by the severe rod of princely justice in our realm. Ye do in the meantime neglect your husbandry, whereby ye must live: your substance and catall is not only spoiled and spent upon unthriftes, who but for this your outrage know no mean nor way to be fedde: your houses falle in ruin, your wives are ravished, your daughters defloured before your own faces, your goods that ye have many long years laboured for lost in an hour and spent upon vagabonds and idle loiterers. Your meat is unpleasant, your drink unsavoury, your sleep never sound, never quiet, never in any safety. What must befal to your children hereafter when your own living is thus through your own folly brought to penury and famine. . . .

What shall be said of you an hundred years hereafter when cronycles shall report that a certain portion of the English people called Devonsheir men and Cornishmen did for popery (which if God be God will long ere that day be utterly confounded and defaced and the name thereof throughout all the Christen world abhorred and detested) did rebel against their natural sovereign lord and king, most earnestly travailing to set forth and publish the true word of God and the true religion of Christ unto them.

B.M. Royal MS., 18 B. xi fol. 1; N. Pocock, 'Troubles connected with the Prayer Book of 1549'; *Camden Society*, new series, xxxvii, 1884, p. 145.

THE COUNCIL TO THE JUSTICES OF THE PEACE OF DEVONSHIRE 1549

This letter and the one following show how the government's attitude to the Western Rebellion changed as its seriousness became apparent.

. . . We require you to traveyll by fayr meannes eyther openly with the hole world, or els apart with the ringleaders by all the best ways you can devise to induce them to retyre to ther houses, putting them and especially the cheff doers among them in remembrance what an onnaturall dealing this is of subjects to rise against ther soveraigne lord. What onkindnes his Majesty may herafter justly conceyve herof sens these things be attempted in his mynorite. Whatt dyshonor and onsuertie to the hole realme may grow by these attemptats. Whatt courage the hearing therof shall administer to the Frenchmen, Scots our enemyes, to putt them in remembraunce that the parts of good and obedient subjects hadd byn ffyrst to have sued for remedie att the hands of ther soveraign lord, and nott to take uppon themselfs the swerd and authorite to redresse as they list, especially those maters which being allredye established by a law and consent of the hole realme can nott (if anything was to be reformed) bee otherwise altered then by a law agayn. By these or such other good words you may fyrst assay to asswage then wherein if you shall not be hable to satisfie them, yett shall you by these meannes somewhat mitigate their furor, and use the meannes you possably can best devyse to stay the comyng of gretter nombers unto them, and in the mean tyme putt your selfs with such of your tenaunts and servants as you best trust, secretly ordered to attend such further direction as our very good lord, the lord pryvey seall, who is now in journey towards you, shall farthar prescribe as for the delay of a tyme for th'execution of the statute. Of the shepe and cloth we have written more amply to you by our former letters, and this eftsones requiring you to joyn wysely and manly together in these things, we bydd you hartily farewell. From Syon. To Sir Thomas Denys, Peter Courteney and Antony Harvy, Justices of the Peace in Devon, xxvith of June 1549.

S.P. Domestic Edward VI, vol. vii, 42; N. Pocock op. cit. p. 12.

THE COUNCIL TO LORD RUSSELL 1549

Frome my L. protector and the Cosell to my L. Pryvie Seall, lieutant to the Kynge's Majestie in the west pties.

... Where ye declare that thoccasyon of being able to levie so fewe in Somersetshire is the evil inclynation of the people, and that there are amongs them that do not styck openly to speak such traterous words agaynst the kyng and in favour of the trayterous rebells. Ye shall hang two or three of them, and cause them to be executed lyke traytors. And that wilbe the only and the best staye of all those talks.

As to them that maketh dyverse excuses and will not serve the kyngs Majestie, ye shall cause them to be noted espially the chiefe doers, and in your retorne they may be ordered according to theyr deserts. Though ye think proclamacons can do no great good, so as we wrote unto you made, yet they may do you some good. Hurt they can do none. ... We do lyke well yor ordering of the ringleaders, and recon no lesse then you do that sharpe justice must be executed upon those sondrie traytors which will learne by nothing but by the sword.

Frome Westminster the xxviith of Julii.

Inner Temple Petyt MS., 538, vol. 46, fol. 444; Pocock op. cit. p. 40.

'KETT'S DEMANDS BEING IN REBELLION' 1549

The only surviving copy of the articles headed as above, has attached to it the names of the representatives of twenty-two hundreds in Norfolk, together with those of Suffolk and the city of Norwich.

1. We pray your grace that where it is enacted for inclosyng that it be not hurtfull to suche as have enclosed saffren grounds for they be gretly chargeablye to them, and that from hensforth noman shall enclose any more.

2. We certifie your grace that where as the lords of the manours hath byn charged with certe fre rent, the same lords hath sought meanes to charge the freholders to pay the same rent, contrarye to right.

3. We pray your grace that no lord of no mannor shall comon uppon the Comons.

4. We pray that prests frome hensforth shall purchase no londs neyther ffre nor Bondy, and the lands that they have in possession may be letten to temporall men, as they wer in the fyrst yere of the reign of Kyng henry the vii.

5. We pray that Redeground and medowe grounde may be at suche price as they wer in the first yere of Kyng henry the vii.

6. We pray that all marshysshe that ar holden of the Kyngs majestie by ffre rent or of any other, may be ageyn at the price that they wer in the ffirst yere of King henry the vii.

7. We pray that all Bushells within your realme be of one stice, that is to sey, to be in mesure viii gallons.

8. We pray that prests or vicars that be not able to preche and sett forth the woorde of god to hys parisheners may be thereby putt from hys benyfice, and the parisheners there to chose an other or else the pateron or lord of the towne.

9. We pray that the payments of castillward rent, and blanche fferme, and office lands, which hath been accostomed to be gathered of the tenaments, where as we suppose the lords ought to pay the same to ther balyffs for ther rents gatheryng, and not the tents.

10. We pray that noman under the degre of a knyght or

esquyer kepe a dowe howse, except it hath byn of an ould anchyent costome.

11. We pray that all ffreholders and copieholders may take the profights of all comons, and ther to comon, and the lords not to comon nor take profights of the same.

12. We pray that no Ffeodorye within your shores shalbe a counceller to eny man in his office makyng, wherby the Kyng may be trulye served, so that a man beeng of good consyence may be yerely chosyn to the same office by the comons of the same sheyre.

13. We pray your grace to take all libertie of lete into your owne hands whereby all men may quyetly enjoye ther comons with all profights.

14. We pray that copiehould land that is onresonable rented may go as it dyd in the first yere of Kyng henry vii and that at the deth of a tenante or of a sale the same lands to be charged with an esey ffyne as a capon or a resonable some of money for a remembraunce.

15. [We pray that no] prest [shall be a chaplain] nor no other officer to eny man of honor or wyrshypp but only to be resydent uppon ther benefices whereby ther parysheners may be enstructed with the lawes of god.

16. We pray thatt all bonde men may be made ffre for god made all ffre with his precious blode sheddyng.

17. We pray that Ryvers may be ffre and comon to all men for fyshyng and passage.

18. We pray that noman shallbe put by your Esthetory and Ffeodarie to ffynde eny office unless he holdeth of your grace in cheyff or capite above £10 a year.

19. We pray that the pore mariners of Fyshereme may have the hole profights of ther fyshyngs as purpres grampes whalles or any grett fyshe so it be not prejudiciall to your grace.

20. We pray that evry propriatorie parson or vicar havyng a benefice of £10 or more by yere shall eyther by themselves or by some other persone teche pore mens chyldren of ther paryshe the boke called the cathakysme and the prymer.

21. We pray that it be not lawfull to the lords of eny mannor to purchase londs frely and to lett then out ageyn by copie of court roll to ther gret advaunchement and to the undoyng of your pore subjects.

22. We pray that no proporiatorie **parson** or vicar in consideracon of advoyding trobyll and sute betwyn them and ther pore parishners whiche they daly do procede and attempt shall from hensforth take for the full contentacon of all the tenthes which nowe they do receyve but viiid. of the noble in the full discharge of all other tythes.

23. [We pray that no man under] the degre of [esquye] shall kepe any conyes upon any of ther owne frehold or copiehold onles he pale them in so that it shall not be to the comons noysoyns.

24. We pray that no person of what estate degre or condicion he be shall from hensforth sell the adwardshyppe of eny chyld but that the same chyld if he lyve to his full age shall be at his owne chosyn concernyng his marriage the Kyngs wards only except.

25. We pray that no manner of person havyng a mannor of his owne shall be no other lords balyf but only his owne.

26. We pray that no lord knyght nor gentleman shall have or take in ferme any spirituall promocion.

27. We pray your grace to gyve lycens and aucthorite by your gracious comyssion under your grett seall to suche comyssioners as your pore comons hath chosyn, or to as many of them as your majestie and your consell shall apoynt and thynke mete, for to redresse and reforme all suche good lawes, statutes, proclamacions, and all other your procedyngs, whiche hath byn bydden by your Justices of your peace, Shreves, Escheatores, and others your officers, from your pore comons, synes the first yere of the reigne of your noble grandfather King henry the seventh.

28. We pray that those your officers that hath offended your grace and your comons and so provid by the compleynt of your pore comons do gyve onto these pore men so assembled iiiid every day so long as they have remayned ther.

29. We pray that no lorde knyght esquyer nor gentleman do graze nor fede eny bullocks or shepe if he may spende forty pounds a yere by his lands but only for the provicion of his howse.

By me Robt Kett   Thomas Cod

By me Thomas Aldryche

B.M. Harleian MS., 304, fol. 75 (**36,** p. 48).

NICHOLAS SOTHERTON: THE COMMOYSON IN NORFOLK 1549

Nicholas Sotherton's eyewitness account was written from the viewpoint of the gentry. It emphasises the element of class conflict in the rebellion.

They appoynted a place of assemblye amonge them in an oken tre in that place, which they bordid to stand on. Uppon which two at ye first did none come but Kett and the rest of the Gouvernours where the people oute ofwer admonishid to beware of their robbinge spoylinge and other theyr evil demeanors and what accompte they had to make. But that lyttil prevailid for they cryid out of the Gentlemen as well for what they would not pull downe theyr enclosid growndis, as allsoe understood they by letters found emonge theyr servants how they sowt by all weyes to suppres them, and whatsoever was sayde they would downe with them soe that within a ii or iii wekes they had sopursuyd the Gentlemen from all parts that in noe place durst one Gentleman keepe his house but were faine to spoile themselves of theyr apparrell and lye and keepe in woods and lownde placis where no resorte was: and some fledd owte of the countrye and gladd they were in theyr howses for saving of the rest of theyr goods and cattell to provide for them daiely bred mete drinke and all other viande and to carry the same at their charge even home to the rebellis campe, and that for the savinge theyr wyves, and chydren and sarvants.

All other provicon they gott by force out of the cytie and commanded every cytezin to bee to them assistant, setting their face to bee the kings ffreinds and to defend the Kings Laws soe impudent were they now become: yea now they would noe more been advertizid by their Governours but theyr Governors must concent to them and by this farr had they not only all Gentyllmen and yeomen att theyr commandment but for the most of Estimacion in the cyttie whereuppon dyvers of the best cytezins with theyr wyves, children, were faine to depart the cittye for that they would by noe meanis obey them and spare up their occupyeng and otheyr theyr substance in secret wyse which understandid, from thenceforth were accompid of the rebellis as Traytors and they in the Campe made Havock of all they could gett. . . . when the state of the cyttie began to bee in most mysserable case, that all men looked for utter destruction both of lyfe and goods . . . and the Gentyllmen they tooke they browte to the tree of Reformacion to bee seene of the people to demande what they would doe with them: where some cryide hang him and some kill him and some that heard noe word criyd even as the rest even when themselvis being demandid why they criyd answerd for that theyr fellows afore did the like, and indeede they did presse theyr weapons to kyll some of those Gentyllmen browte to them which they did of such malice that one Mr Wharton being garded with a Lane of men on both sydes from the said tre into the cyttie they pricked him with theyr spears and other weapons on purpose to kill him had they not had greate helpe to withstand theer malice and creweltye, and further the rest of the Gentyllmenne imprisnid they fettrid with chenis and Locks and pointid divers to ward them for escapinge and in the meane tyme with Kett's authority both Constables and other officers enforcid with theyr company to keepe the Gates that the cytezins shuld not soe fast range furth the cyttie as allsoe that noe Gentyllmenne shuld escape.

B.M. Harleian MS.,1576, fol. 564.

WILLIAM PAGET TO PROTECTOR SOMERSET 1549

*William Paget was one of Somerset's closest advisers. This letter written
on 7 July 1549 is one of a series in which Paget warned the Protector
of the dangers of his policy.*

I told your Grace the trouthe, and was not believed: well,
now your Grace seithe yt what seythe your Grace? Mary, the
King's subjects owt of all discipline, owt of obedience, caryng
neither for Protectour nor King, and much lesse for any other
meane officer. And what is the cause? Your own levytie, your
softnes, your opinion to be good to the pore. I knowe, I saye,
your good meaning and honest nature. But I saye, Syr, yt is
great pitie (as the common proverbe goeth in a warme summer)
that ever fayre wether should do harme. Yt is pitie that your
so muche gentlenes should be an occasion of so great an evell as
ys now chaunced in England by these rebelles . . . Consider, I
beseeche youe most humbly, with all my harte, that societie in
a realme dothe consiste and ys maynteyned by meane of
religion and lawe . . . Loke well whether youe have either lawe
or religion at home, and I feare youe shall fynde neither. The
use of the old religion is forbydden by a lawe, and the use of the
newe ys not yet prynted in the stomaches of the eleven of twelve
partes in the realme, what countenance soever men make
outwardly to please them in whom they see the power restethe.
Now, Syr, for the lawe: where ys it used in England at libertie?
Almost no where. The fote taketh upon him the parte of the
head, and comyns ys become a kinge, appointing condicions
and lawes to the governours, sayeng, 'Grant this, and that, and
we will go home' . . . I knowe in this matter of the commons
very man of the Counsayle hath myslyked your procedings,
and wyshed it otherways.

B.M. Titus MS., fol. 111; *Cal. S. P. Domestic Edward VI*, vol. viii, 4.

SIR THOMAS WYATT'S SCHEME FOR A LOCAL MILITIA 1549

Wyatt's scheme for a militia to protect the government, following the rebellions of 1549, was described by his son George.

... my father, and divers of good sort (for it concerned ye nobillitee and Gentlemen many waise) concideringe hereupon conceavid that the most suer and proper remedie for this headstronge mischife would be to strengthen ye Kings part with a power of ye choise of his most able and trusty subjects, which might upon a very short warninge in a reddiness, wel armed and ordered against all sudden attemptes, either at home or abrode, and whereby he might not doubt to use without danger his other subjects armed and trained ... against any mightie prince that should make invitation upon this realme. ...

This thinge thus in general was movid and propounded to ye Lord Protectors grace then beinge and to divers others of their Honours of ye privie Cousell then unto ye King and was so greate likinge aproved and alowed of, but not concluded unto, either for ye newnes of ye thinge, or for that it was not at that season thought so covenient to have ye subietes armed, whereof ye greater numbers were evel affected to ye religion then professed, or for that some divition then beinge amongst thes that bare ye sway, some hindered that that others liked of. Whereupon, my Father, notwithstandinge partly for his private exercise and partly that he might have sum thinges reddy for this purpose when a better opertunitie might serve ye first waye not taking place, conceived that he with sum of his familiars and companions at many martial bankets, men that had seen and experienced muche in their travels and servese abrode and at home, might doe suwhat that should not be unworthy their travel. ... Thus for the better accomplishinge of his millitary exercise did distribute amongst themselves the sundry parts of this business to those that were best acquainted with the same. Which after was by ye rest so used and perfected by one and mo consent and opinion in such sort as yt grew to a large volume. ...

B.M. Wyatt MS., 17; (**18,** p. 49; **94,** pp. 55–8)

THE TOWER CHRONICLE 1554

'The Chronicle of Queen Jane, and of two years of Queen Mary'
is a pocket diary written by an officer in the royal service, resident in the
Tower of London at the time of Wyatt's Rebellion.

The said Wyat, with his men, marched still forwarde all along
to Temple barre, also thoroghe Fleete Street, along tyll he
cam to Ludgate, his men going not in eny goode order or
array. It is saide that in Fleet street certayn of the lorde
treasurer's band, to the nomber of ccc men, mett theym, and
so going on the one syde passyd by theym coming on the other
syde without eny whit saying to them. Also this is more
strandge: the saide Wyat and his company passyd along by a
great company of harressyd men, which stoode on both
sydes, without eny withstandinge them, and as he marched
forwarde through Fleet street, moste with theire swords
drawne, some cryed 'Queen Mary hath graunted our request,
and geven us pardon'. Others said, 'The quene hath pardoned
us'. Then Wyat cam even to Ludgate, and knockyd calling to
come in, saying, there was Wyat, whome the quene had
graunted their requestes; but the lorde William Howard
standing at the gate, saide, 'Avaunt, traytour! thou shalt not
come in here'. And then Wyat awhill stayed, and, as some say,
rested him apon a seate at the Bellsavage gate; at last, seeing
he coulde not come in, and belike being deceaved of the ayde
which he hoped out of the cetye, retourned backe agayne in
arraye towards Charing crosse, and was never stopped tyll he
cam to Temple barre, wher certayn horsemen which cam from
the felde met them in the face; and then beganne the fight
agayne to waxe hote. . . .

B.M. Harleian MS., 194; *Camden Society*, vol. xlviii, 1850, pp. 49–50.

THE PROCLAMATION OF THE EARLS 1569

In this proclamation, issued at Darlington on 16 November, the earls used the cause of catholicism to rally the north. Similar proclamations were issued at Staindrop and Richmond. They all emphasised the earls' determination to restore the 'ancyent customes and usages' in religion.

Thomas, Earl of Northumberland and Charles, Earl of Westmoreland, the Queens most trewe and lawful subjects, and to all her highness people, sendeth greeting:—Whereas diverse newe set up nobles about the Quenes Majestie, have and do dailie, not onlie go about to overthrow and put down the ancient nobilitie of this realme, but also have misused the Queens Majesties owne personne, and also have by the space of twelve years nowe past, set upp, and mayntayned a new found religion and heresie, contrarie to Gods word. For the amending and redressing whereof, divers foren powers doo purpose shortlie to invade thes realmes, which will be to our utter destruction, if we do not ourselves speedilie forfend the same. Wherefore we are now constreyned at this tyme to go aboute to amend and redresse it ourselves, which if we shold not do and forenners enter upon us we shold be all made slaves and bondsmen to them. These are therefore to will and require you, and every of you, being above the age of sixteen years and not sixty, as your dutie towards God doth bynde you, for the settinge forthe of his trewe and catholicke religion; and as you tender the commonwealth of your countrie, to come and resort unto us with all spede, with all such armour and furnyture as you, or any of you have. This fail you not herein, as you will answer the contrary at your perils. God save the Queen.

B.M. Harleian MS., 6990, fol. 44. Sir C. Sharpe, *Memorials of the Rebellion of 1569*, London 1840, p. 42.

SIR RALPH SADLER TO SIR WILLIAM CECIL 1569

In this passage of a report to Cecil from York on 6 December, Sadler explained why Sussex could not trust his forces in open conflict with the rebels.

I perceive Her Majesty is to believe that the force of her subjects of this country should not increase, and be able to match with the rebels; but it is easy to find the cause. There are not ten gentlemen in all this country that favour her proceedings in the cause of religion. The common people are ignorant, superstitious, and altogether blinded with the old popish doctrine, and therefore so favour the cause which the rebels make the colour of their rebellion, that, though their persons be here with us, their hearts are with them. And no doubt all this country had wholly rebelled if, at the beginning, my Lord Lieutenant had not wisely and stoutly handled the matter. If we should go to the field with this northern force only, they would fight faintly; for if the father be on this side, the son is on the other; and one brother with us and the other with the rebels.

Cal. S.P. Domestic, Addenda, 1566–79, vol. xv, 77.

THE EXAMINATION OF THE EARL OF NORTHUMBERLAND 1572

This is the Earl of Northumberland's own account of the purposes and planning of the rebellion, given in answer to a series of questions put to him by Lord Hunsdon in 1572, when he had been handed over by the Scots. It reveals his hesitancy in entering the conspiracy and shows the extent to which he acted at the instigation of others. The first section transcribed here is Northumberland's account of what happened after the conspirators had received Norfolk's message not to stir.

Then old Norton and Markenfeld came to me and said we were already in peril, through our often meetings, and must either enter the matter without the Earl, or depart the realm; and it would be a great discredit to leave off a godly enterprise that was looked for at our hands by the whole kingdom, many of whom would assist us. I bade them take time to consider; they were away 14 days, and then returned with other gentlemen of the bishopric, and some belonging to the Earl, who were forward in the matter. I objected that my Lord President suspected us, and would not let us escape; but I offered to write to the gentlemen of the country to know their mind. They answered coldly and that stopped us awhile. I wished to consult the Earl of Derby, Queen of Scots and Spanish ambassador. The first did not answer; the other two thought it better not to stir.

Then our company was discouraged. I left my house on a false alarm, and went to Lord Westmoreland's on my way to Alnwick. I found with him all the Nortons, Markenfeld, his two uncles, the two Tempests, John Swinburne, and Sir John Nevill, all ready to enter forthwith. We consulted; my Lord, his uncles, old Norton, and Markenfeld were earnest to proceed. Fras. Norton, John Swinburne, myself, and others thought it impossible, so we broke up and departed, every man to provide for himself. Lady Westmoreland, hearing this, cried out, weeping bitterly, that we and our country were shamed for ever, and that we must seek holes to creep into. Some departed, and I wished to go . . . but when I found I could not get away, I agreed to rise with them.

When did you first enter into this conspiracy? Ans., We first began to talk of these matters when the Duke went in displeasure from Court to his house in London, and it was bruited in Yorkshire that the Council was wonderfully divided about the succession, that the Duke and other noblemen had retired to their houses, and that the realm would be in a hurly-burly; so I sent to the Duke and assembled my friends, to know their inclinations. I and many gentlemen intended to join the Duke, if the quarrel were for reformation of religion or naming a successor, but not to hazard myself for the marriage. This I fear made my enemies about Her Majesty pick a quarrel with me. On the Duke's repair to court, hearing that the reports about naming a successor were untrue, I sought to forbear to stir. . . .

What was the intent and meaning of the rebellion? Ans., Our first object in assembling was the reformation of religion and preservation of the person of the Queen of Scots, as next heir, failing issue of Her Majesty, which causes I believed were greatly favoured by most of the noblemen of the realm. I hoped my Lord Leicester, and especially Lord Burghley, with his singular judgment, had by this time been blessed with godly inspiration to discern cheese from chalk, the matters being so evidently discoursed by learned divines, and they have sway about the Prince, and would bring Her Majesty to the truth; but being deceived, I can only pray God to indue her and them with His grace to know and fear Him aright.

Cal. S.P. Domestic, Addenda, 1566–79, vol. xxi, 56; Sharp op. cit., p. 189.

Bibliography

ORIGINAL SOURCES

Chapters 1 and 2

The attitude of Tudor governments to rebellion can best be studied through the more important propaganda works of 1536 and 1549. Among these are:

Richard Morrison, *A Remedy for sedition concerning the true and loyal obeysance that commons owe unto their prince*, Berthelet, 1536.
Richard Morrison, *A Lamentation in which is shewed what ruin cometh of seditious rebellion*, Berthelet, 1536.
John Cheke, *The Hurt of Sedition how grievous it is to a commonwealth*, J. Daye and W. Seres, 1549.

The anthology in *English Historical Documents* provides a comprehensive survey of contemporary attitudes to social obligations and to rebellion (**82**). For a discussion of the impact of puritanism on the notions of the Great Chain of Being and the body politic as a living organism see M. Walzer's *The Revolution of the Saints* (**44**).

Chapter 3

The best account of the Cornish Rising of 1497 is in The Anglia Historia of Polydore Vergil, ed. Denys Hay, *Camden Society*, third series, 1950, vol. lxxiv (**82**, p. 133). Later accounts, such as Bacon's were based on Vergil, who can be treated as a reliable source since he wrote not many years after the events he described. The London chronicle, which is in the Cotton manuscripts in the British Museum, Vitellius A xvi, is printed in C. L. Kingsford, *Chronicles of London*, Clarendon Press, 1905. The only recent account of the rising is in A. L. Rowse's *Tudor Cornwall* (**35**).

Edward Hall's *Chronicle* provides the most useful account of the Amicable Grant. A number of the reports to Wolsey from the provinces are printed in the *Letters and Papers of Henry VIII*, vol. iv

(I). The fullest modern account of the resistance to the grant is in (**27**); (**21, 26, 45**) are also valuable.

Chapter 4

The main body of documentary material on the Pilgrimage of Grace is conveniently assembled in the *Letters and Papers of Henry VIII*, vols. xi and xii (1). In 1890 M. Bateson printed the important documents relating to the examination of Robert Aske in full in the *English Historical Review*, vol. v.

A comprehensive and completely indispensable account of the Pilgrimage was published by M. H. and R. Dodds in 1915 (**13**). It is based on a very careful and painstaking analysis of the State Paper material. More recent accounts have paid more attention to the secular aspects of the rising (**11, 12, 32**). The rising by Sir Francis Bigod, 'the reformer and eccentric pilgrim', has been treated definitively by Professor Dickens in his study of early northern protestantism (**10**). M. E. James has illuminated the decline of northern feudalism in a number of articles (**63–66**). Professor Knowles has analysed the relations between the pilgrims and the northern monasteries (**16**).

Chapter 5

The only full contemporary description of the Western rebellion is by John Hooker, who was an eye-witness of the seige of Exeter. It is detailed and vividly written. There are several versions of it, the most easily available being that in Hooker's *Description of the City of Exeter*, which was published by the Devon and Cornwall Record Society in two volumes in 1919 (Preface and Index 1947). Hooker was twenty-three at the time of the rebellion. He had been educated at the school kept by Dr John Moreman, the Vicar of Menheniot (**doc. 12,** article 11) and then at Oxford. He had been converted to protestantism when visiting Strasburg where he met Peter Martyr and his bias is evident in his narrative of the rebellion.

Nicholas Pocock's Troubles connected with the Prayer Book 1549, *Camden Society*, new series, vol. xxxvii, 1884, is a useful collection of sources. Somerset's reply to the rebels can be found in Foxe's *Acts and Monuments*, vol. v and Cranmer's in his *Works*, vol. ii. There is no satisfactory recent account of the rebellion but (**34**), the only full narrative, prints a number of important sources. There is a shorter account of the rebellion in (**35**).

Chapter 6

The only eyewitness account of Kett's Rebellion is 'The Commoyson in Norfolk 1549' by Nicholas Sotherton. This is the most important source for the rebellion. The sole surviving copy is in the Harleian Manuscripts in the British Museum. Nicholas Sotherton, whose father had been mayor of Norwich in 1539, was assessed on £17 worth of goods in the subsidy of 1576 and he was then one of the richest men in his parish. He was an alderman from that year until his death in 1587.

In 1575 Alexander Neville one of the younger secretaries of Archbishop Parker, was the first to publish an account of the rebellion, *De Furoribus Norfolkiensium Ketto Duce*. Parker was the son of a Norwich worsted weaver and lived all his early life in East Anglia. He had visited the rebels camp in 1549 and the ecclesiastical historian John Strype maintained in his Life of the Archbishop, published in 1711, that 'he supplied the author with many instructions and remarks, while he was writing, being himself so well acquainted with the subject' (**6,** p. 38). Both Neville's account and Holinshed's in his Chronicles are coloured by the same prejudice as Sotherton shows against the rebels. A statement of the case for the commons and a perceptive analysis of 'covetousness' as the cause of the rebellion, in Hugh Latimer's last sermon before Edward VI, is printed in *English Historical Documents* (82, p. 354-6).

The fullest account of the rebellion based on these sources was published in 1859 (**36**). More recently judicial records have been used to throw light on the local economic factors which caused the rebellion (**50, 75**) and the rebels demands have been briefly analysed in the context of the English Reformation (**12**) and the Tudor economy (**30**).

Chapter 7

The only detailed contemporary account of Wyatt's Rebellion is by John Proctor, a Tonbridge schoolmaster, who in his patriotic treatise *The Historie of Wyate's Rebellion*, intended, by showing that it was a heretical movement, to present 'the lamentable image of hateful Rebellion for the increase of obedience'. Proctor's work is reprinted by E. Arber in *An English Garner*, London, 1877–96, vol. viii. There are shorter accounts of the rebellion in the Greyfriars Chronicle, *Camden Society*, liii, 1852, the Tower Chronicle,

Camden Society, xlviii, 1850, and in Holinshed's *Chronicles*. It is the only Tudor Rebellion to have received comprehensive scholarly treatment in recent years (**18**). There are also accounts in, (**29, 45**).

Chapter 8

A large proportion of the state papers relating to the Northern Rebellion are in print and can be found in the *State Papers Domestic, Addenda*, 1566–79, Sir Ralph Sadler's *State Papers and Letters*, ed. A. Clifford, Edinburgh 1809, and the *Cecil Manuscripts*, Historical Manuscripts Commission. There are also some important manuscript sources, such as Humbertson's survey of the estates of the attainted earls, made in 1570, in the Public Record Office. In 1840 Sir Cuthbert Sharp printed a very useful volume of documents from the Bowes Manuscripts, which contains many of Sir George Bowes letters written in the course of the rebellion, his memorandum on the rebellion and the rebel proclamation. In 1846 J. Raine printed the depositions made in the court of Durham respecting the rebellion, in the *Surtees Society*, vol. xxi. In 1887 H. B. McCall printed and analysed the material in the Bowes papers concerned with the executions following the rebellion (**68**).

Although the sources are more comprehensive than for any other Tudor rebellion no full study of the revolt of the earls has been made: but (**23**) and (**32**) throw much light on it. There are a number of short accounts in recent works, of which the most useful are those in (**20, 31, 45, 46**).

SECONDARY SOURCES

1 Allen, J. W. *A History of Political Thought in the Sixteenth Century*, Methuen 1928.
2 Baumer, F. L. *The Early Tudor Theory of Kingship*, Yale U.P. 1940.
3 Bean, J. M. W. *The Estates of the Percy Family 1416–1537*, Oxford University Press 1958.
4 Beresford, M. W. *The Lost Villages of England*, Lutterworth Press 1954.
5 Boynton, L. *The Elizabethan Militia*, Routledge & Kegan Paul 1967.
6 Brook, V. J. K. *A Life of Archbishop Parker*, O.U.P. 1962.

7 Collinson, P. *The Elizabethan Puritan Movement*, Cape 1967.
8 Cross, C. *The Puritan Earl*, Macmillan 1966.
9 Cruickshank, C. G. *Elizabeth's Army*, 2nd edn. O.U.P., 1966.
10 Dickens, A. G. *Lollards and Protestants in the Diocese of York*, O.U.P. 1959.
11 Dickens, A. G. *Thomas Cromwell and the English Reformation*, English Universities Press 1959.
12 Dickens, A. G. *The English Reformation*, Batsford 1964.
13 Dodds, M. H. and Dodds, R. *The Pilgrimage of Grace and the Exeter Conspiracy*, C.U.P. 1915.
14 Elton, G. R. *The Tudor Constitution*, C.U.P. 1962.
15 Hill, J. E. C. *Economic Problems of the Church*, O.U.P. 1956.
16 Knowles, Dom D. *The Religious Orders in England*, vol. 3, C.U.P. 1961.
17 Laslett, P. *The World we have lost*, Methuen University Paperbacks 1965.
18 Loades, D. M. *Two Tudor Conspiracies*, C.U.P. 1965.
19 Lockyer, R. *Henry VII*, Longmans 1968. (Seminar Studies in History).
20 Lowers, J. K. *Mirrors for Rebels*, Berkeley, California, 1953.
21 Mackie, J. D. *The Earlier Tudors*, O.U.P. 1952.
22 Maconica, J. K. *English Humanists and Reformation Politics*, O.U.P. 1965.
23 Menmuir, C. *The Rebellion of the Earls of Northumberland and Westmorland, 1569*, Newcastle, 1907.
24 Neale, Sir John, *Queen Elizabeth*, Cape 1934.
25 Neale, Sir John, *Elizabeth I and her Parliaments*, 2 vols., Cape 1953.
26 Pickthorn, K. W. M. *Early Tudor Government*, vol. 2: *Henry VIII*, 2nd edn. C.U.P. 1951.
27 Pollard, A. F. *Wolsey*, Longmans 1929; (Fontana paperback 1965).
28 Powicke, Sir Maurice, *The Reformation in England*, O.U.P. 1941 (Oxford paperback, 1961).
29 Prescott, H. F. M. *Mary Tudor*, 2nd edn. Eyre & Spottiswoode 1952.
30 Ramsey, P. *Tudor Economic Problems*, Gollancz 1963.
31 Read, C. *Mr Secretary Cecil and Queen Elizabeth*, Cape 1955.
32 Reid, R. R. *The King's Council of the North*, Longmans 1921.
33 Ridley, J. *Thomas Cranmer*, O.U.P. 1962.

34 Rose-Troup, F. *The Western Rebellion of 1549*, Smith, Elder 1913.

35 Rowse, A. L. *Tudor Cornwall*, Cape 1951.

36 Russell, F. W. *Kett's Rebellion in Norfolk*, Longmans 1859.

37 Shaw, H. *The Levellers*, Longmans 1968.

38 Stone, L. *The Crisis of the Aristocracy*, O.U.P. 1965.

39 Tawney, R. H. and Power, E, ed. *Tudor Economic Documents*, vol. 3, Longmans 1924.

40 Tawney, R. H. *The Agrarian Problem in the Sixteenth Century*, Longmans 1912.

41 Thirsk, J. ed. *The Agrarian History of England*, vol. 4. C.U.P. 1967.

42 Tillyard, E. M. W. *The Elizabethan World Picture*, Chatto & Windus 1943; (Peregrine paperback 1963.)

43 Thomson, J. A. F. *The Later Lollards*, O.U.P. 1965.

44 Walzer, M. *The Revolution of the Saints*, Weidenfeld and Nicolson 1966.

45 Wernham, R. B. *Before the Armada*, Cape 1966.

46 Williams, N. *Thomas Howard, Fourth Duke of Norfolk*, Barrie and Rockliff, 1964.

47 Woodward, G. W. O. *The Dissolution of the Monasteries*, Blandford 1966.

48 Zeeveld, W. G. *Foundations of Tudor Policy*, Cambridge, Mass., 1948.

ARTICLES

49 Bateson, M. 'The Pilgrimage of Grace and Aske's Examination', *English Historical Review*, 1890, pp. 330–48, 550–73.

50 Bindoff, S. T. 'Kett's Rebellion', *Historical Association*, 1949.

51 Bossy, J. 'The character of Elizabethan Catholicism', *Past and Present*, 21, April 1962.

52 Brooks, F. W. 'The Council of the North', *Historical Association*, 1953.

53 Collinson, P. 'The Godly: Aspects of popular Protestantism in Elizabethan England', paper presented to the *Past and Present* conference on popular religion, July 1966.

54 Dickens, A. G. 'Sedition and Conspiracy in Yorkshire during the later years of Henry VIII', *Yorkshire Archaeological Journal*, xxxiv, 1939.

55 Dickens, A. G. 'Some popular reactions to the Edwardian Reformation in Yorkshire', *Yorkshire Archaeological Journal*, xxxiv, 1939.

56 Dickens, A. G. 'The First Stages of Romanist Recusancy in Yorkshire', *Yorkshire Archaeological Journal*, xxxv, 1941.

57 Dickens, A. G. 'Robert Holgate', *Borthwick Papers*, 8, St Anthony's Press, York, 1955.

58 Elton, G. R. 'The Tudor Revolution: a reply', *Past and Present*, 29 December 1964.

59 Fisher, F. J. 'The growth of the London food market', in *Essays in Economic History*, vol. 1, ed. E. M. Carus-Wilson, Edward Arnold 1954.

60 Gay, E. F. 'The Midland Revolt and the inquisitions of depopulation of 1607', *Trans. Roy. Hist. Soc.*, xviii, 1904.

61 Hill, C. 'The many-headed monster in Tudor and Stuart England, in *From the Renaissance to the Counter-Reformation*, ed. C. H. Carter, Cape 1966.

62 Hoskins, W. H. 'Harvest fluctuations and English economic history 1480–1619', *Agricultural History Review*, xii, part 1, 1964.

63 James, M. E. 'The Murder at Cocklodge', *Durham University Journal*, lvii, no. 11, March 1965.

64 James, M. E. 'Change and continuity in the Tudor North', *Borthwick Papers*, 27, St Anthony's Press, York, 1965.

65 James, M. E. 'A Tudor Magnate and the Tudor State', *Borthwick Papers*, 30, St Anthony's Press, York, 1966.

66 James, M. E. 'The first Earl of Cumberland (1493–1542) and the decline of northern feudalism', *Northern History*, i, 1966.

67 Kerridge, E. 'The movement of rent 1540–1640', *Economic History Review*, vi, 1953.

68 McCall, H. B. 'Executions after the Northern Rebellion', *Yorkshire Archaeological Journal*, xviii, 1887.

69 Phelps Brown, E. H. and Hopkins, S. U. 'Seven centuries of the prices compared with builders' wage rates', *Economica*, 1956; in *Essays in Economic History*, vol. 2, ed. E. M. Carus-Wilson, Edward Arnold 1954.

70 Pound, J. F. 'The social and trade structure of Norwich 1525–75', *Past and Present*, 34, July 1966.

71 Reid, R. R. 'The rebellion of the Northern Earls', *Trans. Roy. Hist. Soc.*, 1906.

72 Reid, R. R. 'The political influence of the north parts', in *Tudor Studies*. ed. R. W. Seton-Watson, Longmans 1924.

73 Russell, C. S. R. 'Arguments for religious unity in England 1530–1650', *Journal of Ecclesiastical History*, xviii, 1967.

74 Stone, L. 'Social mobility in England 1500–1700', *Past and Present*, 33, April 1966.

THESES

75 Hammond, R. J. 'The social and economic circumstances of Kett's Rebellion', London Ph.D., 1934.

76 Loades, D. M. 'Popular subversion and government security in England during the Reign of Mary I', Cambridge Ph.D., 1961.

77 Schofield, R. S. 'Parliamentary lay taxation 1485–1547', Cambridge Ph.D., 1963.

78 Smith, A. H. 'The Elizabethan gentry of Norfolk: office holding and faction', London Ph.D., 1959.

79 Smith, R. B. 'A study of landed income and social structure in the West Riding of Yorkshire in the period 1535–46', Leeds Ph.D., 1962.

ADDENDA

80 Bean, J. M. W. *The Decline of English Feudalism*, Manchester U.P. 1968.

81 Bowker, M. 'Lincolnshire 1536: Heresy, Schism or Religious Discontent', in *Studies in Church History*, ed. D. Baker, ix, 1972.

82 Bush, M. L. 'The Problem of the Far North: a Study of the Crisis of 1537 and its Consequences', *Northern History*, vi, 1971.

83 Davies, C. S. L. 'The Pilgrimage of Grace Reconsidered', *Past and Present*, 41, 1968.

84 Dickens, A. G. 'Secular and Religious Motivation in the Pilgrimage of Grace', in *Studies in Church History*, ed. G. J. Cuming, iv, 1967.

85 Elton, G. R. *Policy and Police*, C.U.P. 1972

86 Haigh, C. *The Last Days of the Lancashire Monasteries and the Pilgrimage of Grace*, Chetham Society, xvii, 1969.

87 Hill, C. *The World Turned Upside Down*, Temple Smith, 1972.

88 Ives, E. W. 'The Genesis of the Statute of Uses', *English Historical Review*, lxxxii, 1967.

89 James, M. E. 'Obedience and Dissent in Henrician England: The Lincolnshire Rebellion 1536', *Past and Present*, 48, 1970.

90 Jones, W. P. D. *The Tudor Commonwealth*, Athlone Press 1970.

91 Jordan, W. K. *Edward VI: The Young King*, Allen and Unwin, 1968.

92 Jordan, W. K. *Edward VI: The Threshold of Power*, Allen and Unwin 1970.

93 Lehmberg, S. E. *The Reformation Parliament*, C.U.P. 1970.

94 Loades, D. M. *The Papers of George Wyatt*, Camden Society, fourth series, 5, 1968.

95 MacCaffrey, W. *The Shaping of the Elizabethan Regime*, Cape, 1969.

96 Palliser, D. M. *The Reformation in York*, Borthwick Papers, 40, St. Anthony's Press, York 1971.

97 Scarisbrick, J. J. *Henry VIII*, Eyre and Spottiswode, 1968.

98 Simpson, A. *The Wealth of the Gentry*, C.U.P. 1963.

99 Smith, R. B. *Land and Politics in the England of Henry VIII*, O.U.P. 1970.

100 Thomas, K. *Religion and the Decline of Magic*, Weidenfeld and Nicholson 1971.

101 Tyler, P. 'The significance of the Ecclesiastical Commission at York', *Northern History*, ii, 1967.

102 Williams, C. H. *English Historical Documents*, v, 1485–1558, Eyre and Spottiswode 1967.

162

Index

Numbers preceded by the letter M refer to a map on the page mentioned.

165

Index